Introductory Theology

Introductory Theology

Zoltan Alszeghy and **Maurizio Flick**

Dimension Books • Denville, New Jersey

First American Edition 1983
by Dimension Books Inc.

American ISBN 0-87193-198-2

Table of Contents

Prefatory Note

A master chef once told me that he always began the course of instructions to potential chefs by explaining the way to handle and crack an egg. It seemed a bit elementary. He replied, "You might just as well start at the beginning."

When we begin to study theology, it is important to know what it is. It is therefore essential to know the ingredients that go into the dish we call theology. We can look at theology as the new student sees it — from the point of view of the classes he or she must attend Usually, following the pattern of some years, theological studies are divided into biblical, dogmatic or systematic, and moral. These are the major areas admitting of many subdivisions.

The field of biblical studies centers on the word of God. To approach these studies the student will need in minimum terms a good translation of the Bible and an adequate, up-to-date commentary on Sacred Scripture. Chapter 7 will provide a bibliography of the works to which a student ought to have access in order to build a foundation in the knowledge of Sacred Scripture.

The word *dogma* signifies a religious truth established by revelation and defined by the Church. Dogmatic theology is the systematic study of religious truth as the Church has articulated it over her lifetime. Two essential tools for this study are the documents of Vatican Council II and the collection of important doctrinal statements of the Church, the *Enchiridion Symbolorum Definitionum Declarationum*, better known as the Denzinger after the editor of the first edition. Chapter 7 has a section on other works essential to the study of Church doctrine.

Moral theology is the study of the application of Christian doctrine to daily living. It is the scientific understanding of the implications of the Gospel for each believer.

Some additional courses that will fill out the curriculum are Church History, Canon Law, and Liturgy. Also included will be studies in applied theology: pastoral and spiritual.

One tool that is reemerging as a highly useful one in the study of theology is the so-called manual. This, once common, recently discredited and now reviving, aid to study gives the student an overall view of a particular area of theological concentration, e.g., grace, sacraments, or the Church. It shows the history of the discussion, the major arguments and principal magisterial statements, together with the various theological positions held yesterday and today.

The manual provides a skeleton around which future theological work can be built. It is true that the skeleton is not the whole body. But it is equally exact that the weight of the body cannot be sustained without a healthy bone structure. Theological formation must begin with an understanding of the major areas of theological discussion, what questions have been raised, what answers offered, and in what general direction the Church has moved historically in facing that specific problematic. Once this is grasped and integrated into one's understanding, further development is possible. To race into theological speculation without an adequate formation or grasp of the history of the issue and the Church's response to the matter in question, is to dissipate precious energies.

To this point the Sacred Congregation for Catholic Education directed attention with the publication of the April-June issue of *Seminarium* in 1976. The issue is dedicated to the question of theological textbooks today. The following quotation is from the English introduction to the volume: "Both the 'Ratio fundamentalis institutionis sacerdotalis' (in n. 88) and the recent document 'The Theological Formation of Future Priests' (in n. 126), in their treatment of methodology and the practical didactic side of the teaching given in seminaries, have emphasized the need to have good textbooks for the various disciplines. The reason for this recommendation is clear. All teaching, in order to be truly fruitful and useful for the studies of the ministerial priesthood, must be not only informative but formative as well. That is to say, it must be given and structured in such a way as to be able to communicate to the students a philosophico-theological wisdom which is unified, solid, complete, and secure. Naturally, it also must be practically able to be assimilated, which means it must be clear, and the essentials must be present in its formulations.

"Such requirements and prerogatives for teaching imparted to future priests should be normally secured through the use of the didactic helps called 'manuals.' These are textbooks which are usually prepared by professors whose value cannot be questioned and which are built upon specific teaching experience and on the common doctrine of the Church. This means that doctrine of faith and morals which expresses the 'depositum fidei,' which in turn creates the unity and unanimity of the individual members of the ecclesial community and which must be taught, preached, and present in every place and in every moment of the Church's earthly pilgrimage" (p. 211).

The document goes on to point out that in recent years, following the Council, manuals fell from favor. This is true for many reasons, often not unconnected with the quality of the manuals themselves. Students found themselves turning more and more to periodical literature. And although the exchange of fresh ideas was augmented, it became increasingly apparent with the passage of time that a structured, systematic grasp of theology was becoming a victim of the theological ferment. The document notes that "a new state of affairs has been established from which there is obvious suffering imposed not only upon the efficacy of study and teaching, but even on pastoral practice and the entire life of the Church" (p. 211).

Hence the encouragement given the new students to become familiar with some manual or series of books directed toward classroom use and its presumed systematic study. Chapter 7 provides further information in this regard.

This book, *Introductory Theology*, is first of all an explanation of what theology is. It helps the student define the subject. But it is particularly helpful to the new student of theology or one who is seeking to understand the changes that have taken place, and are taking place, in the world of theological study. It is essentially a clear presentation and summary of what is new in theological method following Vatican Council II.

The footnotes for the most part document the authors' position and show where they have turned to draw inspiration and example. In this translation, wherever possible, the English language title is supplied if the work is cited in an Italian translation. The rest, however, are kept in the original language edition as they are found in the Italian *Come si fa la teologia*.

For the newcomer to theology the seventh chapter with its reference to source books is most important. For this reason I have taken the liberty of providing the English-language source books readily available in the United States. For example, where the authors indicate an Italian translation of the Bible and Italian commentaries on Sacred Scripture, I have substituted English-language works. This translation also enlarges Chapter 7 to include some more recent titles and material useful to the student of theology today.

Donald W. Wuerl

1

A Lexicographical Approach to Theology

What is theology?

It is not possible to answer this question on the basis of etymology by saying that theology is the study or discussion of divinity. In this perspective, theology would not be distinguishable from theodicy, theosophy or other mental activities that no one today would call theological. It is clear that, in the course of history, the term "theology" has received a specific meaning that does not come solely from the philological root.

But neither is historical research sufficient to define the precise meaning of this word. In fact, it has been used in such different ways that one historian concludes the documentation he has gathered with the observation that the Greek or Latin word "theologia," used in the ancient texts, can only in particular and infrequent cases be translated in modern languages as "theology."[1]

We believe, in fact, that semantics must follow only the linguistic usage in which words are applied. According to a self-evident formula (but nevertheless a true and important one), a word signifies what those who utter it mean, neither more nor less.

A very correct way of proceeding, therefore, is adopted by a philosopher of religion, who begins the definition of theology with the following words: theology is what Christian theologians, especially Catholic ones, designate with this term.[2] We, too, will try to gather the characteristics that are understood, particularly in Catholic ambience, when the word "theology" is used. In other words, the *principle of identification* according to which we determine the meaning of the word "theology" is *linguistic usage*.

Theology, an Activity of Faith

Common usage does not limit the meaning of theology to a "discussion about God." This is seen by the fact that very often today, the

word "theology" is followed by a genitive (e.g., of history, of liberation, of preaching), which has meaning only if it is supposed that
theology is not just a question of God and his attributes.

Nor is the term applied to all reflection on the various realities *in
their relationship with God:* the various philosophical theories, in fact,
are clearly distinguished from theology, even when they consider
their subject matter in relation to an Absolute.

The reference to real or alleged divine manifestations is not sufficient to make a discussion a theological one. There exists a vast body
of scientific writing describing and explaining the religious beliefs of
various peoples. These works, which belong to religious ethnography
or to the history of religions, are not included by anyone among
"theological" works. Even if the subject is Christian religious doctrines, the study of religions is not yet theology. Such a treatment is
considered theological only when the author intentionally presupposes that the phenomena described are based on a real divine revelation, reechoed, preserved, and developed in a true community of
salvation. It is generally held that persons who study the Christian religion are "theologians" only *if they have the faith,* and if they study
the Christian religion with a prior understanding of faith. At a time
when the whole of European culture was imbued with the faith, this
assertion seemed so evident that is was only rarely explicitly developed.[3] When in the nineteenth century, stress on the absolute objectivity of science raised the question whether the theologian's
adherence to the faith did not compromise the scientific value of
theology, the popes reaffirmed repeatedly that theology does not exist
without faith.[4] Moreover in the present-day discussion on the meaning and the limits of the dependence of theological research on the
Magisterium, it is taken for granted on both sides that the theologian
is a person of faith.

We will not examine, at this moment, the reason why in actual
fact the attitude of a Buddhist or of an atheist who studies (even with
perfect objectivity) the teaching of the Catholic Church, differs profoundly from the attitude of the believing Catholic, who (also with the
same objectivity) dedicates himself or herself to the same study. We
will merely note an expression of the Church's understanding of what
she considers "theology": *theology is an activity of faith,* the theologian is a believer, one who has the faith, or rather, is possessed by
faith.

What faith is will be analyzed by theology itself. However, right
from the beginning of our theological investigation we can postulate

an approximate notion of it. We must, in fact, avoid quite a common rationalistic distortion, according to which "to believe" means only, or mainly, to accept a series of affirmations ("God is One and Three," "There are seven sacraments") on the authority of God who reveals. Without denying the intellectual aspect of faith, we must remember that faith is an existential attitude based on dialogue and rooted in a fundamental option, which permeates the believer's whole existence, in response to the call of a personal being. In this way we understand the importance of the description given by Vatican II, according to which "the obedience of faith" is an attitude in which "man freely commits his entire self to God, making "the full submission of his intellect and will to God who reveals, and willingly assenting to the Revelation given by him.'"⁵

Believers are Possessed by Faith

We said that the believer, more than possessing faith, is *possessed by faith*. In fact, as the Council continues, "before this faith can be exercised, man must have the grace of God to move and assist him; he must have the interior helps of the Holy Spirit, who moves the heart and converts it to God, who opens the eye of the mind and 'makes it easy for all to accept and believe the truth.' "⁶ Let us note that the Christian faith, even if unconsciously, has a Trinitarian structure: it adheres in full trust and obedience to the Father, participating in the filial attitude of Christ, by virtue of the Spirit, who makes us capable of discovering not only the reasonableness, but also the beauty of his full acceptance that is filled with a call to action.

Faith is not, and cannot be, an isolated attitude. It is realized only *in the context of the structured behavior* of a Christian life. Therefore, right from the beginning of the institutional organization of the sacred sciences, teachers of theological methodology have reminded scholars of what might be called the ascetic requirements of this study. "Idcirco, summopere cavendum est ei, qui quaerit scientiam, ut non negligat disciplinam," Hugh of St. Victor, the author of one of the first studies in theological methodology, once observed.⁷

The Second Vatican Council, again, quotes the text of St. Bonaventure, which stresses the spiritual and existential context of theological study;⁸ recently, too, theological reflection has tried to elaborate the reasons internal to this proposition that might be called living. Faith, as a dialogic attitude toward God, must not be considered just as the threshold one must cross in order to study theology. It is the "living" area in which this study can develop. We will have occasion to recall how all theological work, even in its strictly intellectual aspect (as the critical interpretation of ecclesial life, in the light of the sources, in tension toward future formulations, postulated by the environment), is possible only by virtue of that connaturality as a result of which not only is the Christian message "declared" (from outside) but also "understood" (from inside). This connaturality is a fruit of living faith, understood as a permanent option to dialogic opening to God.

Adherence to God is not, however, an affective attitude, deprived of content, precisely because God's life is not just a blind force, but also a thought. To adhere to God means also (and essentially) to accept his way of seeing the universe. The conformity of created thought with the Divine Word is realized through acceptance of the Word God has willed to communicate to us for our salvation. God's self-communication to us, as a result of which we are raised above our creatureness and are brought into the intimacy of the Trinity, presupposes an awareness of the divine plan, through which God's self-communication is realized. In the present order of salvation, in which God has spoken to us several times and in different ways, and in recent times definitively by means of his Son (cf. Heb. 1: 1–2), perfect adherence to God through faith inevitably implies also the *acceptance of revealed* assertions.

According to St. Paul, if the events proclaimed in the kerygma are not real, the proclamation of Christ by preachers and the adherence to Christ by the faithful are "in vain," that is, void of content, foundation, and living force (cf. 1 Cor. 15: 3–19). The content of the message is not at all considered a negligible element. In fact, anyone who proclaims objective propositions different from the Gospel, once it has been proclaimed, is thereby separated from Christ, becoming "anathema" (Gal. 1: 8–9). Already toward the end of the apostolic era, there was talk of a deposit of doctrine, delivered once and for all, which must be guarded in its noetic identity (1 Tim. 1:10; 6:20; 2 Tim. 2:9–19; 4:3–5; Titus 1, 9; 2 John 9, 11). Certainly, the content of Christ's preaching develops in contact with new situations not directly clarified by Christ (cf., e.g., the controversy over the admittance of uncircumcised pagans to baptism, Acts 15). But great care was always taken to show how the new applications were in continuity with the deposit, by comparing them with the common faith of the apostles and relying on the charismatic action of the Holy Spirit. The reason why an assertion is imposed as a postulate of subjective faith is not its power to arouse enthusiasm, but its connection with revelation, once it has been made to the Church.

Therefore the formula "to believe in," which expresses the personal and dynamic orientation of the faith, was accompanied right from the Synoptics by the formulas "to believe that" and "to believe (some thing)," which refer to assertions accepted as true because they were "said" by God. The intellectual aspect of faith is not the only one, nor the main one, but it is indispensable for Christian existence and is the horizon of all theological study.

Having defined theology as "an activity of faith," we cannot avoid the conclusion that faith (understood as a subjective attitude and as an acceptance of objective assertions) precedes theological study. A serious question is raised here. Is not this conception a *form of fideism*, disapproved by the Church (cf., e.g., DS 3033)?

Faith Is a Rational Act

Faith must appear as a *rational act*, and therefore the reasons for credibility must be recognized, at least implicitly (DS 3009–3010). If it were not so, Christians could not be called to account for the hope that is in them (1 Pet. 3:15). But certain knowledge can exist even without a scientific proof; in fact, our firmest persuasions are not actually based on proofs. The certainty with which a child, returning after a long absence, recognizes his or her parents at the airport, the certainty with which, in a successful marriage, one partner rejects a slander put forth with regard to the other partner, are not preceded by argumentations, yet they do not imply doubts. It is a question of an immediate perception of a set of indications, which can have no other reasonable explanation than the truth of an assertion, which is somehow grasped intuitively in the indications themselves.

The structure of an act of faith is very similar. A message is perceived. Its properties (harmony, elevation, depth) are seen. The figure of Jesus Christ, the center of this message, is contemplated, described in such a way that it cannot be invented, but must correspond to a reality, unique and superhuman. The message is perceived not abstractly, but in the historical context of internal effects (conversion, charity, peace, fortitude in tribulations) and external ones (a set of extraordinary facts, beginning from Israel's exodus from Egypt, through the Resurrection of Christ, to the miraculous cures of recent times). These, at least as a whole, show clearly that in the message and its propagation there is "God's hand." Anyone who listens to the message and perceives its properties, its content, and the signs that accompany it, recognizes in it (in the light of grace) the voice of God, just as children recognize the voice of a parent speaking to them in the darkness.

Such an immediate and intuitive recognition, though not the *fruit of explicit reasoning*, may be resolved and justified by means of reasoning. An expert, who, at the first glance, recognizes in a painting the work of some great master, can enumerate subsequently the criteria that prove the validity of the attribution. If the expert is not capable of doing so, his or her intuition will remain doubtful. In the same way, by and large, believers, too, can reflect on the certainty of their own faith and can account for its reasonableness. Not every believer, of course, has the intellectual formation necessary to make this critical analysis in a convincing way. But basic theology, at least in its "apologetic" aspect, has been specifically constituted as a science that shows, in a methodical, speculative, and universal way, that the message of Christianity is worthy of faith because it is of divine origin. Such a justification concerns itself not only with the subject presented (the testimony of Christ, the signs of his mission, the foundation of the Church), but also with the human subject to whom revelation is addressed, and it highlights the fact that the doctrine corresponds to the deep aspirations, intuitions, and needs of humans.

It must be quite clear, however, that faith is *not the conclusion* of scientific research. If faith were the fruit of a proof, it would no longer be a free adherence, and therefore it would not be worship of God (DS 3008). No scientific proof, moreover, can lead to that firm certainty, which is typical of faith. Believers must be ready to give even their lives for their faith; to admit that revocation of the assent of faith may be justified, already destroys the assent of faith. On the contrary, the proof based on the interpretation of religious texts going back to a remote antiquity, can never give such a certainty: a scientist must always remember that it is a fundamental noetic principle of every science to remain open to correctives, with which other studies may go beyond the conclusions admitted at present.

The condition of the theologian is, therefore, equidistant from rationalism (intellectual adherence to the message, based on the clearness of the arguments) and from fideism (irrational adherence or at least adherence that does not have a rational basis). It presupposes faith, the rationality of which is perceived, but which consists in free adherence to the word of God, who reveals the salvific mystery of his own life and, in the light of this mystery, gives a new intelligibility to our existence and to our world.

We will understand theology better as an "activity of faith" if we distinguish faith from two similar, but different attitudes, that is, from the *certainty of one who sees* and from the attempt to *utilize faith to complete knowledge.*

What we said about the firmness of faith is, in fact, misunderstood if one concludes that believers are so dazzled by the light of grace that they are insensitive to all subjective doubt. It must be very clearly recognized that it is possible to have a sincere and strong faith and yet be tempted in faith and be aware of objections for which at the moment there is no solution. A *difficulty* of faith is not a *doubt.* A "difficulty" is an instance, which seems to contradict an assertion of faith, accepted as a problem to be solved, in a person convinced (for reasons recognized as definitively valid) that to believe is reasonable, and resolved to accept the Christian message as the norm of one's own existence. "Doubt" is an instance contrary to faith, accepted as probably valid, so much so that the person suspends assent to the Christian message and accepts the necessity of further deliberations with regard to the option of faith.

The distinction is by no means an arbitrary one, and it is regularly used in everyday life. No one can solve always and at once all the objections made to one's own convictions; and no one abandons one's own well-grounded convictions because of a question that momentarily cannot be answered. Conservative doctors, who, at the end of the nineteenth century, denied that the cause of some diseases was to be sought in microbes, had arguments; those who, on the strength of empirical proofs, admitted the existence of pathogenic living germs, were not yet able to solve at once all the arguments to the contrary. In those who did not know the empirical proofs, the arguments brought forward by the traditional school against the existence of microbes, had the force of a doubt; in those who were convinced, through experiments, of the harmful effects of certain microbes, the same arguments were reduced to mere difficulties.

The same distinction must be admitted also with regard to faith. Faith, though it can be justified rationally, is neither knowledge nor a vision. It rests, in fact, on the word of God, which carries us to a horizon different from, and superior to, that of sensible experience, and beyond the evident truths posed by reason. Therefore faith always remains essentially "obscure," even if the reasons for credibility are clear. Sacred Scripture compares the Word of God, on which the faith rests, to a "lamp shining in a dark place, until the day dawns" (2 Pet. 1:19). The paradoxical tension between lucidity and obscurity is a constant also of the theologians' condition. The life of faith, also for them, as for every believer, though it is a gift of grace, is not an exceptional mystical state, but is an attitude similar to the one with which a person, having complete confidence in another person, accepts as true, on the other's testimony, an affirmation unlikely in itself.

The obscurity of faith remains a characteristic of the Christian condition, which is not removed even by the study of theology. It is a mistake to think that all doubts can be settled and all difficulties dispelled in the course of study, in proportion to the various theological doctrines that are examined.

On the contrary, it often happens that it is the analytical studies themselves that call attention to the seeming contradictions of the faith and stress the contrast that exists between faith statements and the rational arguments deeply rooted in one's cultural background. The joy and peace that flood the life of many fervent Christians are not the fruit of theological study, but rather gifts of the Spirit, who responds to humble and persevering prayer and to that selfless love that gives itself for the good of one's neighbor. Intellectual effort may be said to help and sustain the certainty of subjective faith, in the sense that the theologian, when he or she has completed required studies, sees the whole synthesis of the message of salvation. The unity and harmony of this synthesis constitute a new argument for the truth of the faith and also give a meaning to existence (while all other explanations of reality lead to absurdity).[9]

If faith itself is not knowledge, then theology, an activity of faith, must be considered *a source of subsidiary information for knowledge.* It is true that theology discovers the ultimate direction of reality and indicates a way for complete development of mankind; but it exercises this function precisely when it does not consider it the principal motive of theological study. In this field, too, we can apply the Gospel words: "Seek first his kingdom and his righteousness, and all these things shall be yours as well" (Matt. 6:33).

A scholar who wished to exploit the message of faith to make up for, complete, or correct the gaps in empirical and rational knowledge, and who therefore studied theology to collect information about created reality in itself, or (what is more frequent in our times) to construct programs of immediate action for the liberation, the progress, and the development of society, would be misusing the word of God and end up embroiled in a scientism. The study of theology is justified not by the desire to know some object (even if in the light of the word of God), but by the aspiration to listen to the divine message of salvation (even if in relation to the empirically known cultural environment in which we must operate).

In this content a statement made by the theologian Dietrich Bonhoeffer to the students of the Protestant theological school of Berlin University in the autumn of 1933 is very significant. The situation of students of Protestant theology in Germany in those years was similar to that of Catholic theologians today: political events had brought forth the hope of a "secular" revival, lessening the value of the action of the Christian churches in the eyes of a good many. So Bonhoeffer's text is extraordinarily relevant today.[10]

Anyone who would study with equal interest other subjects, medicine or law, for example, merely because it is necessary to study something to prepare for a profession — the young professor admonished — should not study theology. Those who are attracted by the word of God should dedicate themselves to theological study. This attraction does not consist of a special experience of a divine call. It is manifested in readiness to think of God, or his word, and his will, and in the satisfaction found in meditating on the divine law day and night (Ps. 1:2). Therefore, the conception of theology as an activity of faith brings with it the readiness to develop, also intellectually and with the technical procedures of a science, the content of the word of God, in a sober, serious, and responsible way.

It is clear that theologians may be keenly interested in philosophical, ethical, pedagogical, and social problems; those who did not bring these interests into their study would be poor theologians. But they must study deeply as theologians the various questions posed by different human problems. They must find their impetus and the norm of their research in the faith.

Theology, the Science of Faith

Lexicographical usage of current language presupposes that theology claims to be a science. Even those who fundamentally exclude the validity of knowledge based on revelation and referring to objects over which there is no empirical control, distinguish a book of theology from a collection of religious hymns, moral exhortations, or mystical contemplations. To be called theological, a work must refer to *given sources*, it must use a *method of exact communicability*, and it must present *verification principles* with regard to its own affirmations. In this very wide sense, theological study certainly has a "scientific" character. It tries to "rationalize" faith, not by proving its truth on the basis of rational evidence, but by formulating precisely the assertions that are postulated as true faith, and by justifying these assertions, that is, by showing clearly their relationship with faith itself.

Theology Differs from Other Sciences

There is no doubt that theology differs from all other sciences, both natural and human. There is a certain tension between the two characteristic properties of the "science of faith" — the "believing" character and the "rational" one — a tension that has caused deep reflection in the Church.[11] Vatican Council I, in the grip of fideism and rationalism, had to explain explicitly the characteristic function of theology as the search for an understanding of the faith. "Reason, enlightened by faith, when it seeks sedulously, piously, and soberly, obtains, with God's help, a certain understanding of the mysteries, which is extremely fruitful, both from the analogy of things he knows naturally, and from the connection of the mysteries with one another, and with man's ultimate end" (DS 3016).[12]

The Council considers "reason" as the subject of theological work, that is, man's natural cognitive faculty, the source of all science. Reason, in theology, puts itself at the disposal of "faith." In the first place, it takes the objective content of the message of salvation as truth. In this way, it is "enlightened by faith." Furthermore, reason adapts itself in its operation to the subjective way postulated by faith to scrutinize the mysteries of salvation. The three words used by the Council, "sedulous, pious, sober," characterize this way. "Sedulous" indicates diligence in meditating on the divine word; "sober" puts us on guard against the temptation of wishing to go beyond the specific limits of human reason when it faces a mystery. The requirement of "piety" is particularly interesting. Semantically, for Vatican Council I, the term "pious" conveys a religious attitude, brought forth by a meeting with the sacred, and takes on concrete shape in respectful and trusting love.

It is clear, therefore, that, according to Vatican Council I, reason, when applied to theological work, must be enlightened by faith not only for the acceptance of objective assertions, guaranteed by revelation, but also for a subjective orientation with regard to values discovered by faith. Theologians study the message of salvation, not in order to gain possession of it but, recognizing its transcendence, to put themselves in its service in order that the message may have its full development.

The condition of the theologian, in fact, cannot be adequately described, if we consider only what he or she does. The function of the theologian calls for a transcendental influence of God. The expression "Deo dante" indicates, in fact, that a divine intervention is necessary. This intervention is, of course, different from the so-called ordinary concurrence through which God bestows being and activity on every creature. With these two words, the Council introduces a subject that was greatly developed in the patristic past, was still present in medieval theology, especially monastic theology, and is almost completely passed over in silence today: the opening to divine influence, which inspires the will and enlightens the intellect.

Patristic theology, right from the time of the Alexandrian school, expressed this truth when it spoke of the "gifts of the Holy Spirit." Later the philosophical category of "enlightenment" dominated. When the Scholastic theory of knowledge abandoned the Augustinian theory of enlightenment, the conviction regarding the necessity of a grace to study theology survived only in the affirmation of a supernatural "habitus," characteristic of theological cognition. The Council dispenses with all these theoretical explanations. The necessity of divine help for the development of theology does not depend, in fact, on the various explanations mentioned, but is an immediate consequence of the fact that theology depends on faith. Since faith is essentially a work of grace, its intellectual development, too, is promoted by an internal and supernatural divine influence, that is, by grace, in its twofold function of healing and elevating.

Theological activity results in a certain understanding of divine reality, in its being and operation (God's internal life, the incarnation, salvation). The Council calls these themes of faith "mysteries," indicating that they are not accessible to human experience, but are, in fact, completely different from naturally known reality (cf. DS 3015). So the very meaning of the assertions that refer to the mysteries is understandable only through the triple analogy: correspondence between the natural and the supernatural order, harmony of the various mysteries with one another, subordination of individual gifts to the ultimate end of man saved by Christ.

The effort of theological work aims, therefore, at answering not the question "an sit" (whether it is) but the one, "quid sit" (what it is) The Council is reserved in promising "some understanding" of the mysteries, since an explanation by means of analogy can never be exhaustive. In this way it reechoes the teaching already contained in Lateran Council IV, according to which it is not possible to indicate a similarity between God and creation without pointing out that there exists an even greater dissimilarity (DS 806).

Vatican Council II studies in a special way a particular aspect of the teaching of Vatican I, that is, the function of divine operation within humans. According to the Council, God exercises an interior influence on the human psyche, which makes possible, realizes, and conditions the whole activity of faith. We find this emphasis on the primacy of grace, in the first place, with regard to faith itself. The Council recalls that to accept revelation with faith, "man must have the grace of God to move and assist him; he must have the interior helps of the Holy Spirit, who moves the heart and converts it to God, who opens the eyes of the mind and makes it easy for all to accept and believe the truth."[13] The Council extends the necessity of grace also to the fruitful intellectual development of faith: "The same Holy Spirit constantly perfects faith by his gifts, so that revelation may be more and more profoundly understood."[14]

Nevertheless, the influence of "grace" certainly does not replace any stage of the psychological process through which man reaches an intellectual conviction. Enumerating the human factors of progress in the understanding of faith, the Council indicates the activity of reason in the first place. "There is a growth in insight into the realities and the words that are being passed on ... through the contemplation and study by believers, who ponder these things in their hearts...."[15] In this way, "as the centuries succeed one another, the Church constantly moves forward toward the fullness of divine truth."[16]

The "scientific" aspect of theology, in Vatican II, appears rather as an unquestionable premise of operational choices, e.g., in the context of the freedom of theological research[17] and in the teaching of dogma in seminaries.[18] The problem has already been studied in documents of the Holy See, which aimed directly at guiding theological teaching and research, and which also influenced indirectly the linguistic usage of the word "theology" in the Church.[19]

Theology Is Noetical, Methodical, and Critical

In the cultural environment of Catholicism, theology means, therefore, a noetic, methodical, and critical activity, which presupposes adherence to the Catholic faith. We do not mean, of course, that these elements are explicitly present in the consciousness of anyone who utters the word "theology," but use of the term indicates at least an implicit concept, not thought out, which rises to consciousness when, following the Socratic method, the question is posed why certain expressions of religious thought and not others are designated with the term "theology."

The reaffirmation that the two poles of theology are activity of faith and scientific activity, does not yet solve the question how the two aspects can be united in a living activity. In this connection, there exist various conceptions in theology itself, among which two movements prevail at present.

One, characteristic of Neo-Scholastics, conceives the relationship between faith and reason in theology as follows: it considers the articles of faith the basis of theological study, and it attributes to scientific reason the task of discovering their conclusions, both by determining by a line of reasoning the assertions that follow from the truths of faith, and by showing clearly how one truth of faith may be considered a consequence of other truths. This conception leads to an organic system of truths, and unites in the explanation of theological study the attitude of faith (with which revealed truths are accepted), and that of deductive reasoning (which discovers the logical relationship existing among them).

One may wonder, however, whether this conception does not neglect too much the hermeneutical difficulties that theologians meet with when they try to work out the exact meaning of the articles of faith, and whether this conception does not overemphasize the importance of the doctrinal consequences, which, because they are not directly revealed, are less important in the edifice of faith and therefore should not have attention focused on them in theological work.

At present there seems to prevail another concept of theological reflection, which is perhaps even more traditional than the first one. For this school of thought the principal aim of theology is to understand the faith. This does not exclude interest in conclusions (it is not possible to understand fully a doctrine until the positions that are virtually contained in it are also known). However, research is geared not to "fides quaerens conclusiones," but to "fides quaerens intellectum." The condition of the theologian implies, therefore, a living faith, as a result of which he or she is driven to work out, in a way that is intellectually exact, communicable, and verifiable, the message which in faith is believed to be true.

This conception of theology as the pursuit of an understanding of faith is confirmed by a linguistic usage that is quite widespread, namely to speak of the theology of personalities and groups who never dedicated themselves to methodical and well-thought-out research into the truths of faith. We speak, for example, of the theology of writers, people of action, spiritual movements and, above all, saints. Studies dedicated, for example, to the "theology" of St. Theresa of Lisieux or of Elizabeth of the Trinity throw light on the personal way of conceiving the mysteries of faith and their organic unity, implicitly lived by these personalities, so that their interior attitude to God and to their neighbor becomes understandable, as well as the exterior behavior derived from it. This fact has its importance because it proves that the spoken language itself presupposes a very close relationship between the science of theology and faith as it is lived. Theology is not, therefore, the search for conclusions that follow from clearly and distinctly formulated assertions, but rather the tendency "to explain" the faith, which is already accepted implicitly and globally, in a way that unfolds its richness. Christian existence is not a premise of theology, but theology in germ. The professional theologian expresses clearly and examines reflectively a set of assertions preconsciously present in every Christian life.

This shows already that theology is not a superfluous and extraneous addition to Christian existence. The "science of faith" is nothing but the methodical and critical exposition of theology put into practice, and therefore it corresponds to a requirement of life itself. This will become clearer when we show that the starting point of theology is precisely ecclesial life.

Theology, an Ecclesial Function

For centuries Western thinkers described human cognition as a process through which a subject receives in himself or herself the image of an object. This fundamental schema was used also in the analysis of the cognition of faith, since divine revelation was often considered almost solely a means to bring to the mind of the knowing subject the image of the object revealed. The great innovation in reflection on language was the discovery that the subject-object schema is inadequate. It is a question, in fact, of an abstraction, which never occurs in isolation. All cognition is possible, in fact, since the subject is immersed in a community in which he lives his meeting with reality. We must take this discovery into account also when describing the condition of the theologian. For this reason, in fact, many theorists of theological method agree with Karl Barth's expression, according to which the theologian "in relation to the word of God and his testimony, is never in a void, but, very concretely, in the community."[20]

We have quoted a statement of a Calvinist theologian, to avoid misunderstandings. The Catholic, reflecting about the ecclesial dimension of theology, thinks immediately of its dependence on the Magisterium. This dependence certainly exists, and we will indicate its function in due time. But it is not the primary and central community element of faith. This is so to the extent that if one begins with this view alone, an organic understanding of the way in which the theologian is integrated in the community of believers becomes almost impossible.

A certain community character of theology already emerges from a mere lexicographical consideration, since theology is commonly called a science. Although it can be debated to what extent any given definition of science can be applied to theology, it is clear, however, that the view that considers science a pursuit carried on within the community, or rather by the community, is fully applicable also to theology. Today, in fact, sciences are not the results of the speculation or experimentation of any isolated eccentric. A publication has a "scientific value" only if it is integrated in that complex cybernetic structure, as a result of which the scientist must take into account the results, opinions, hypotheses, and questions proposed by others, and must make his or her own results, opinions, hypotheses, and questions accessible to others so that they can take them into account.

Science in its totality, with its immense mass of information and processes, does not exist in any individual consciousness, but is an objectivity to which individuals can have recourse to solve new problems. The value of the scientist depends precisely on an ability to benefit from this documentation stored by the collectivity. This presupposes a system of communication, a language, a sharing of intentions and of certain basic views, especially operational ones.

The theologian, therefore, is a member of that "cosmopolis" to which all those engaged in the study of theology belong.

But, for theology (as we pointed out before), *faith* is required; faith, in its turn, is a far more community attitude than science. One has faith, since one is in the community of believers; let us call it Church, disregarding all further specifications of this term. Therefore, the integration of the theologian in the community takes on a depth and a breadth that are not found in any other science. Theologians know they are united with all the other disciples of Christ, not only because they study theology, but also because they believe and recognize that they are called to be children of God. They consider themselves united not only with those engaged in the science, but also with all those who accept the word that they (the theologians) are trying to understand. This depth and breadth of community integration are postulated by the very condition of the theologians because, if they isolated themselves from the community, they would become for this very reason incapable of cultivating their science.

In fact, it is mostly the Church that leads us to faith, since the message in which we recognized the word of God is, in practice, the preaching of the Christian community that surrounds us and into which we have been introduced since childhood; it is the testimony of this community that enables us to recognize Holy Scripture as the word of God.

What is more, it is the Church that offers us the concrete way of carrying out the acceptance of the faith. It invites us to take part in her doxology and promises us that, as we belong to her, we will also receive the Spirit, who is the soul of the community and gives life to all those brought together as members in the community of salvation. The Church also formulates the mental contents, without which we cannot live as real disciples of Christ. In fact, it is through the testimony of the Church (and only through it) that we know what Sacred Scripture is and of what books it consists. Finally the Church interprets the word revealed by God, indicating its meaning with authority (because it is assisted by the Spirit), and developing it far beyond the point at which human reason could arrive if left to itself in the effort of interpretation.[21]

Of course, those who study the Christian religion and do not have the faith will not be able to form a precise idea of it without taking into account the influence of the Church. They will not confess the Christian message as true and salvific precisely because they do not agree to be members of the Church.

Owing to the fact that we live in the Church, we accept, through the testimony of the Church, in the life of the Church, and according to the interpretation of the Church, the word of God as true and as the way to salvation. So the assertions worked out by the science of theology indicate not only what is the doctrinal content of the Christian religion, but also what is the truth that saves us.

Adherence to the community of salvation, in spite of the fundamental note of joyful certainty that one is on the right way, does not exclude at all awareness that the community of salvation, in the present phase, is a people proceeding on its pilgrim way toward salvation. In the perspective of theological existence, this awareness is particularly keen. The individual belongs to the Church, but in a critical way he or she distinguishes what, in the Church, is authentic and what, on the contrary, is the result of a deviation from her founder's intention. This effort to distinguish is necessary for ecclesial life and constitutes the germ of theological activity.

At this point we can accept another element of linguistic usage regarding the term "theology." Whenever the context is not sufficiently clear, we add to the word "theology" an adjective indicating membership of a given Church. Thus we speak of Catholic, Lutheran, Orthodox òr Baptist theology. At present, this denominational indication seems less important to many, since the great lines of demarcation between the various movements cross all denominations horizontally. There are thinkers in all the churches who admit or who reject, for example, the validity of Chalcedonian Christology or the personal immortality of the soul. Yet, the community life of each church considers itself separated from all the others, as is shown, for example, in the great difficulties involved in carrying out eucharistic intercommunion, even on a reduced scale. This is explained by the fact that the faith of the various churches takes on different concrete forms.

Theology, which is the science of faith, must express this diversity, which does not consist so much in admitting or not admitting given assertions as true, but rather in the structure of the whole interpretation of the Christian message.

A description of theology, which emerges from common usage and designates it as an activity of *faith*, the *science* of faith, and a function of *ecclesial* life, could certainly be directed toward a definition that would determine the object, the subject, the sources, of theology. We will not take this path, which has already been well explored by several books on theological methodology. In accordance with our intention to provide an introduction to the "trade" of the theologian, we are interested rather in a genetic interpretation of this activity, and we raise the question, "Where does the study of theology have its starting point?"

Chapter Notes

1. G. Ebeling, "Theologie, Begriffsgeschichtlich," in: *Religion in Geschichte und Gegenwart* (Tübingen, 1962), pp. 754–69. Also *New Catholic Encyclopedia*, vol. 14;

pp. 39–65; *Sacramentum Mundi: An Encyclopedia of Theology*, ed. K. Rahner, 6 vols. (New York, 1960), vol. 6, pp. 233–49.

2. H. Duméry, *Critique et religion, Problèms de methode en philosophie de la religion* (Paris, 1957), p. 259.

3. Cf. e.g. Bonaventure, 3 *Sent.*, dist. 35,q.2 (*Op.* 3,776); Suarez, *De fide*, disp. 3, sect. 11, no. 9. The two greatest theologians of the Scholastic period were St. Thomas Aquinas and St. Bonaventure. Both wrote extensively. Most of the notes in this book that indicate the writings of St. Thomas or St. Bonaventure refer respectively to their works; the *Summa Theologica* (*S.Th.*) and the *Commentary on the Sentences of Peter Lombard* (*Sent.*). Bonaventure (Giovanni di Fidanza c. 1217–74) was a Franciscan and was later given the title "Doctor Seraphicus." Aquinas (Tommaso d'Aquino 1225–74) was a Dominican and is also called the "Doctor Communis" and the "Doctor Angelicus." Suarez (Francisco de Suarez 1548–1617) was a Jesuit theologian who wrote many works, most of which were commentaries on the *Summa Theologica* of St. Thomas Aquinas.

4. Encyclical *Mirari vos* of Gregory XVI 1832, DS 2732; condemnation of Hermes in 1835, DS 2738; Address *Singulari quadam* of Pius IX in 1854, Denzinger-Bannwart 1642 Oath against Modernism prescribed by Pius X in 1910, DS 3547. Church documents referred to in the Denzinger-Schonmetzer collection will always be designated in theological writing by a DS followed by the number given that particular statement in Denzinger.

5. *Dei Verbum*, n. 5: Vatican Council II, *Dogmatic Constitution on Divine Revelation* (November 18, 1965).

6. *Ibid.*, internal quote: Second Council of Orange, can 7: *Denzinger* 377; First Vatican Council, *Dogm. Const. on Catholic Faith*: DS 3005.

7. *Didascalia*, 1, 3, c. 13, *PL* 176, 773: The writings of most of the great teachers and Fathers of the Church up to the thirteenth century are found in the Migne collection of the Fathers, *Patrologiae cursus completus, series latina*, ed. J.P. Migne, 221 vols. (Paris, 1844–1855). Works in this collection are identified as *PL* with a number to indicate the volume and another to locate it within the volume. *PG* designates writings in the *Patrologiae cursus completus, series graeca*, ed. J.P. Migne, 161 vols. (Paris 1857–1866). The *Didascalia* by Hugh of St. Victor (d. 1142) is a guide to the study of theology.

8. *Itinerarium*, Prol. no. 4 (*Op.* 5, 296); Cf. *Optatam totius*, n. 16: Vatican Council II, *Decree on the Training of Priests* (October 28, 1965).

9. This point of view is studies by W. Kasper, in *Einführung in den Glauben* (Mainz, 1972).

10. D. Bonhoeffer, Was soll der Student der Theologie heute tun?, an article published for the first time in the program of lessons at Berlin University in the winter term of 1933, 34; cf. *Gesammelte Schriften* (ed. E. Bethge) 3 (Munich 1960), pp. 243–47.

11. Cf. e.g. M.D. Chenu, *La theologie comme science au XIIIᵉ siècle* (ed. 3, Paris, 1957)

on the Middle Ages; K. Eschweiler, *Die zwei Wege der neueren Theologie* (Augsburgh, 1926) on the nineteenth century; B. Casper, K. Hemmerle, P. Hunermann, *Theologie als Wissenschaft* (Freiburg, 1970) for today's problems.

12. For the analysis of this text, let us follow J. Beumer, *Theologie als Glaubensverständnis* (Würzburg, 1953), pp. 153–88.

13. *Dei Verbum*, n. 5.

14. *Ibid.*

15. *Dei Verbum*, n. 8.

16. *Ibid.*

17. *Gaudium et spes*, n. 59, 62: Vatican Council II, *Pastoral Constitution on the Church in the Modern World* (December 7, 1965).

18. *Optatam totius*, n. 16.

19. Cf., e.g., the encyclical *Aeterni Patris* of Leo XIII, in 1879 (cf. a significant passage in DS 3135), that of Pius XI *Deus scientiarum Dominus* (AAS 23, 1931, 241–80), and the directives given to theologians by Paul VI (cf. *Acta Congressus Internationalis de Theologia Concilii Vaticani II*, Rome, 1968, XIII–XXII, and XLIII–L).

20. K. Barth, *An Introduction to Evangelical Theology*, trans. by G. Foley (New York, 1963).

21. The function of adherence to the Church in the act of faith was already expressed by St. Augustine in his arguments against the Manichaeans: "Ego vero Evangelio non crederem, nisi me Catholicae Ecclesiae commoveret auctoritas . . .": *Contra Epist. Manichaei c. 4, PL* 42, 176.

2

The Starting Point of Theology

The starting point of intellectual activity is always a question that people try to answer. Therefore the exact formulation of the initial question is the central methodological problem of every science.

Any question is formulated by starting with a phenomenon, which in a certain sense is already known, and about which we would like to know something more. To express the question in the form of an interrogative sentence, the known element will constitute its subject; the new knowledge, which we seek, is expressed in the predicate. Thus we ask: What does a certain term mean? What is the use of this object? What is the cause of a specific event. Is this statement true?

The Subject: The Community Life of the Church

The question that forms the starting point of theological research can be expressed in this way: The Community life of the Church, what does it mean? That is, how can it be interpreted, made perfectly intelligible?

In this question, the *subject* is the community life of the Church. It is a question of a phenomenon in which the intellectual content of faith is present, but still in a prescientific state, that is, in such a way that its acceptance does not necessarily imply thoughtful and critical activity. The *predicate* is the exact formulation of this community life, which is found by projecting it on the level of science, that is, by reducing it to communicable and verifiable assertions.

The *answer* to this question will be the scientific exposition of the assertions that must be admitted as true in order to take part authentically in ecclesial life. By a "scientific" exposition, we mean the use of conceptionalized formulation of various affirmations, the proof of a

31

relationship between them and ecclesial life, and the systematic order in which the different propositions must be considered. Theological assertions thought out in this way will be both proved and believed. As the object of critical science, they need verification because they are proposed as the interpretation of ecclesial life as the object of faith; assuming that they belong to ecclesial life, they are, therefore, accepted unconditionally.

On beginning theological research, we do not yet know what will be the subject of the assertions we will obtain from the analysis of ecclesial life. Perhaps, they will all refer to God, considered in his inmost life. Perhaps they will refer to Christ as mediator and savior, or perhaps to humans since they are led to the Father by Christ in the Holy Spirit. In stressing this initial indeterminateness, it is clear that the problem of the starting point of theology is not identical with the problem of the object (or the subject) of theology. The first problem is of interest when theology is considered as an activity to be exercised (which is our point of view); the second one turns on theology considered as a system of truths (classical approach of the usual theological methodologies).

The Community Life of the Church and the Magisterium

In an ecclesiology that tended to identify the Church with the hierarchy, it was easy to reduce the community life of the Church to the teaching of the Magisterium and to approach theological study as an interpretation and defense of papal and conciliar documents. The schema of Neo-Scholastic theses, which often began by quoting the documents of the ecclesiastical Magisterium, strengthened the view that theological research started with the declarations of the Magisterium, which constituted the norm of orthodoxy.

It is clear that theological study cannot ignore these formulas that make up a very important and normative element of ecclesial life. But they are not sufficient in themselves to begin theological work, and far less do they constitute its ultimate basis.

The formulas of the Magisterium alone do not constitute a sufficient launching pad for theological research. These formulas, juridically exact, were created mainly to serve as an identity card for the unity of faith, and can never in themselves alone contain all the riches of revelation. There are aspects of the faith on which the documents of the Magisterium are silent. The authoritatively proposed formulas usually emerge from given historical situations and concentrate on disputed points. They are inevitably one sided. The development of dogma usually proceeded with the enunciation of a true aspect of the Christian message, on which, in the previous phase of teaching, the Magisterium had not yet said anything. When this silence occasioned a new error, the opposite of the previous position, a new formulation, equally one sided, completed the first one. There is a dialectic between the condemnations of Nestorius and Eutyches, between those of Pelagius and the Jansenists, between the definition of papal primacy at Vatican I and the doctrine of episcopal collegiality in Vatican II.

In the struggle to define theologically the faith statement "Christ is the Son of God," various extremes were reached. Nestorius (d. 451) wished to preserve the emphasis on the humanity of Christ. He used the formula that there were in Christ two distinct and not joined natures, one divine the other human. Eutyches (378-454) emphasized the divinity of Christ and eventually denied that the manhood of Christ was of the same substance or being as that of ours. Pelagius, a fifth century theologian, taught that man took the initial and main step toward his salvation on his own. This doctrine the Church judged to negate the need for grace. The Jansenists of the seventeenth century held that man needed grace to such an extent that he is predetermined supernaturally. According to this teaching man needs special grace for any naturally good act. Papal primacy refers to the emphasis placed on the teaching role of the Pope by the First Vatican Council (1869–70). The Second Vatican Council (1962–65) pointed out the place of the bishops in the teaching office of the Church and emphasized the notion of collegiality. In all of these theological tensions there was at work a dialectic that led the Church to clarify the proper understanding of the faith statements that prompted the theological discussion.

These examples show that not only are the documents of the Magisterium insufficient in themselves to start theological investigations, but also that they are already a fruit of it. The Magisterium, in its positions, uses material prepared by theological reflection. For its anathemas, the Council of Ephesus (431) needed the formulas of Nestorius and the refutation of Cyril; the necessity of healing grace could not have been defined without the passionate defense of the goodness of nature made by Pelagius and without the affirmation of original sin by Augustine. To describe the birth of dogma without regard for this theological preparation, and to use definitions as an absolute beginning, are to run the risk of taking the positions of the Magisterium as the fruit of new revelations or of spontaneous generation. The validity of this assertion is not diminished even if councils and pontiffs have sometimes created formulas without the collaboration of theologians. In these cases, the pastors of the Church themselves before teaching with authority, carried out the task of theologians; in the same person, the function of the researcher preceded that of the authentic teacher.

The Magisterium itself, though it often stresses the function that theology has in explaining and defending the teaching of the hierarchy, admits nevertheless that theology also has its own specific mission in preparing its positions. According to Paul VI's explicit teaching, theology is halfway between the faith of the Church and the Magisterium. When it studies more deeply the interpretation of the faith, it informs the hierarchy, and when it sets forth the teaching of the hierarchy, it deepens the faith of the community. Therefore, without theology, the Magisterium would lack the organ necessary to exercise its own office.[1]

The Community Life of the Church as Culture

The tendency to locate the subject of the initial question of theology in a phase prior to the formulas of the Magisterium, is producing significant developments in contemporary theological literature, even though their importance is often not sufficiently stressed. "The only valid starting point for theological reflection is the experience the communities of our time have of God's salvific action";[2] "the starting point of theology is the faith of the Church";[3] "the object of theological research is offered to the theologian by the life of faith of the whole Church."[4]

There is a certain convergence in these statements; but those who know the three theologians we have quoted are aware that their theological methods are profoundly different, right from the starting point. In fact the expressions, "ecclesial experience," "faith of the Church," "life of the Church," are terms of variable meanings and not exactly interchangeable. In formulating the question that constitutes the starting point of theology, in order to construct a proper methodology, we cannot be content with a verbal convergence. We must state precisely what we mean when we speak of "ecclesial life."

Let us start from a concept that is the object of attention in various disciplines today: the concept of "culture."

The term "culture" usually designates the set of interior and exterior forms of behavior (intellectual, affective, productive, and artistic) that distinguish one group of people from another, and are derived from various causes (biological, psychological, environmental, historical). They are reflected in the use of given objects, in the acceptance of given institutions (religious, social, political), and above all in language. The structure of these elements is relatively constant, to such an extent that if one is changed, a corresponding change usually takes place in the others.

Generally, the concept of "culture" is opposed to that of "religious faith"; the same faith, in fact, can be accepted and expressed in various cultures. This distinction can be explained, since in the description of the various cultures, the most easily perceptible elements are often infrareligious phenomena, such as, for example, the way of obtaining food, of defense against enemies, of institutionalizing social relations, and therefore equally compatible with the various religions. On the other hand, it must also be stressed that religious beliefs form a part of culture that is not negligible. In fact, the very religious life of a community constitutes to some extent a "culture" within a culture (a "subculture"). Since it, too, is the result of convictions, appreciations, etc., it is incarnated in customs and institutions that are linked structurally.

If we compare this subculture with other cultural units, it will appear as characterized by a greater internal unity. At least in the great, fully developed religions, the relationship between the various elements is so close that those who belong to these "cultures" respond with a reaction of violent rejection to the introduction of any extraneous element. Owing to this unity, deeply experienced and often also justified intellectually, there will be an inclination to apply to religious culture the category of the "objective spirit." In fact, its structure no longer appears as a mere mass of independent elements that may even be in conflict with one another, but as one "essence," which is manifested in the totality of the various phenomena.

Therefore it seems possible to us to describe the community life of the Church as a "culture," noting a group of characteristic features most often found in communities that live their membership in the Catholic Church with a certain intensity. Of course, we do not exclude the possibility that one or more of these features may be lacking, and vice versa, that they may be found not only outside the Catholic Church, but also outside Christianity.

Anyone who observes the community life of the Church from the outside finds material expressions (cathedrals, paintings, chants, objects of worship), institutional expressions (a liturgical system, a canon law), and a set of customs that appear not only in the field of worship, but also in folklore, in family life, and in social life. There emerges from all this a conception of the world that implies intellectual conviction and affective orientation, which can be described systematically in theological literature. This type of existence implies, as its foundation, the believers' acceptance of their role as disciples of Christ, who is the source of salvation for those who, gathered in his name, try to carry out the Father's will.

The sociologist and psychologist will point out that this set of phenomena is due to the reciprocal interplay of individual convictions and the formative influence of the collectivity that strengthen, complete, and modify one another. The historian will note that the ecclesial reality was formed gradually, through various phases of evolution or involution, in a certain continuity with the movement that began with Christ, in a continuous relationship (of assimilation and rejection) with the environment.

The believer will recognize the constant action of the Holy Spirit, who lives in Christ's Church, and communicates to individuals and to the community a share in the life of the Trinity, thus determining a specific form of human existence. The theologian will add, however, that the Spirit not only adapts himself to the human substratum, and uses it (from this is derived the different expressions of the life of the Trinity in each individual, in each particular community, and in each period), but also does not exclude those weaknesses characteristic of man marked by sin. Therefore, as the Eastern theologians particularly stress, the Spirit, who lives in the Church, undergoes a kenosis, comparable to the kenosis of the Word Incarnate, since his light never disperses, not even in the Church, whose soul he is, the darkness of ignorance and malice. This is so because, until the eschatological fullness, he is hindered in action by human deficiency.

The life of the Church, described and conceived in this way, finds its focal point in doxology, which is realized above all in the liturgical assembly.

The love and worship expressed in doxology imply an operational and affective stance with which the faithful, as individuals and as members of the community, recognize that they need grace, are obliged to gratitude, and are called to faithfulness before God the Savior, who offers them his covenant in Christ. They also imply inseparable recognition and acceptance of membership of the community, as a result of which the faithful commit themselves to the service of one another, rely on the help of others, and are invested with that role that every member of the Church has with regard to those who are outside it.

The intellectual convictions that form the Christian concept of the universe are a postulate of the operational and affective, personal, and intersubjective positions that spring from ecclesial doxology, and are united with it by a psychological and logical tie. For example, it is not possible to have trust in God if one is not convinced that God exists, is powerful, faithful, benevolent; therefore, the authenticity of religious experience calls for the subjective conviction of given theological assertions. And it is not reasonable to have trust in God if the assertions in question are not true; therefore, the validity of religious experience calls for the objective truth of theological assertions.

The Community Life of the Church as a Linguistic Event

It will be easier to discover in the community life of the Church the subject of the question that constitutes the starting point of theological research, if we realize that this life, precisely because it has the nature of a "culture," can also be called a "linguistic event."

Language, according to a rather widespread definition, can be described as a system of verbal or symbolic signs, and of rules for their use, formulated implicitly or explicitly. Reflection on the phenomenon of language has proved definitively that language cannot be considered exclusively as a system of the phonetic communication of previously formed contents. Language is not only the vehicle of the content, but also the form of the very experience through which the content comes into being. In fact, it is a vital form of a person, since we are all influenced by our environment. It might be said that language is nothing but culture, since it becomes observable exactly at the level of phonetic communication.

In the first place, language contains a stock of words that constitute a conventional unit of communication, and through the latter it also implies a system of concepts. It is an illusion to think that each word belonging to a given language always corresponds to another word in all other tongues. Words often have a power of evocation that is not completely translatable. Every individual sees the inexhaustible riches of reality through the conceptual screen of the language in which he or she thinks and speaks.

Language also contains a syntax, by which speech is constructed.

Syntactical rules are closely united with the form of thought, in such a way that the system of sentences is by and large characteristic of the structure of reasoning. A declarative sentence, with which a Greek or a Latin "describes" reality, and the paratactical sentences, with which the Hebrew "narrates" the same reality, inspire, through the architecture of the sentences, a different way of reasoning. One of the main problems, for example, that the English translator of a German essay has to solve is how to break up the long sentence of the original without distorting its meaning.

Finally, language also implies experiences and convictions. Expressions and sentences such as "to treat paternally" (or "paternalistically"), "it's not worth a dime," "a dog's life," "he's no genius," imply opinions on the way fathers treat their children, on the value of a dime, on the treatment meted out to dogs, and on the qualities of genius. These convictions are transmitted by language, even if the individual has not had any direct experience in this connection, and they are based on the collective experience of the community that created its language.[5]

Ecclesial life, based on faith, is a product of speech: its birth and development are unthinkable without the continual proclamation of the word within the community, in the various environments (family, liturgical assembly, scholastic institution) and in all forms of homiletics and catechesis (preaching, teaching, exhortation, and correction). Therefore ecclesial life is more deeply imbued with the characteristics of the language, from which it springs and through which it develops, than other forms of culture in which direct experience has a greater influence.

Since, furthermore, Christian commitment concerns mainly one's "heart," that is, one's inner life, turned, in dialogue and community, toward a personal God, ecclesial life has a special reason to be called a linguistic event. It is realized through a sharing of ideas, conceptual schemata, appreciations, and forms of behavior, through which the community addresses God, and which not only presuppose a language, but also share the characteristics of the language.

The linguistic characteristics of ecclesial life are shown above all in its internal tendency to manifest itself connaturally in a linguistic expression. The living faith of the Christian community bursts out instinctively in the invocation: "Abba! Father!" (Gal. 4:6), and in the testimony: "We cannot but speak of what we have seen and heard" (Acts 4:20). Doxology and preaching, as irrepressible outlets of ecclesial life, express their nature as a linguistic event.

Specific Characteristics of the Ecclesial Linguistic Event

We intend to develop the concept of ecclesial life as a linguistic event only to the extent that it is useful to specify the question that constitutes the starting point of theological study. In fact, looking at the particular characteristics of the linguistic event to which the basic question of theological research refers, we realize why and in what sense it is necessary to ask ourselves how it should be interpreted.

In ecclesial life we are continually coming across formulas that seem obscure to those who are not accustomed to them, and that are so different from the language of everyday life that they call for a certain interpretation even from believers, if they do not want to renounce the unity of their own personal existence.

Father Chenu gathers an interesting series of examples, taken from the language of faith, which need to be explained.[6] What is the exact meaning of the "kingdom of heaven," of which the parables give such different images? To what doctrinal category (juridical, historical, mystical) does the "covenant" belong, which, in the Old and New "Testaments," expresses God's plan? How do we obtain a unified picture of Jesus Christ, who is called King, Son of David, Son of man, servant of the Lord God, Angel of the Apocalypse, God the Savior, the future Judge? What does it mean that Jesus "went down to hell"? Anyone who reads the Bible, follows the liturgy, or meditates on a book of piety, continually meets with similar problems.

The fact that at present the religious language of the Church is different from everyday language is an elementary finding. This normally leads to the conclusion that the liturgical formulas must be updated and homiletic style improved to avoid artificiality. But the speech in which ecclesial life becomes incarnate, will, inevitably and as a result of an internal necessity, reveal a deep difference from all other linguistic phenomena.

The specific nature of the linguistic event constituting ecclesial life can be described as having three properties: it is radically self-implicative, rich in symbols, and bound to linguistic forms of the past.

The first aspect is postulated by the purpose at which the whole community life of the Church aims. The Church is nothing but the response to the word of God, lived in faith. The revealed word of God is addressed to us, not to instruct us directly in an objective way about God and his intimate life, but to bring forth in us an attitude that will please the Father and bring us to salvation. The words with which St. John concludes his Gospel: "These are written that you may believe that Jesus is the Christ, the Son of God, and that believing you may have life in his name" (John 20:31), are applicable to the whole of Revelation and to the whole linguistic event that is the community life of the Church.

This leads us to the specific character of the "language of faith," which we find, in its purest form, in the Church's liturgy.

Studies on language distinguish in every linguistic event three dimensions: expressive, creative, and affirmative.[7] A witness, for example, who states before a court that he saw a person in a given place, expresses his interiority (since he communicates a memory), creates a new situation for the individual who was seen (since he accuses him or frees him from blame), and affirms an element of objective reality. The linguistic type (or literary genre) of an expression depends to a large extent on the prevalence of one of these dimensions. Lyric poetry stresses almost exclusively the author's feelings. In an order, the creative function, which carries with it an obligation, is emphasized. In a scientific assertion everything is concentrated on the conformity of the affirmation with the objective reality. In the spoken language of every day, the three dimensions are mixed indiscriminately.

For the community life of the Church, language is used in a way that characteristically pervades all three of these dimensions. From this point of view, liturgical language is similar to everyday conversation. In liturgical language, however, there clearly prevails *the creative dimension, in its "self-implicative" specification*, which is used, in everyday language, when we say, for example, "I promise you," "I'm sorry," "I congratulate you." In these cases the purpose of speaking is not to inform others about what we think, but to determine actively our situation with regard to others, since we invest ourselves with a given role, creating obligations for ourselves, giving satisfaction, expressing our solidarity. *The prevalence* of this dimension is characteristic of religious language, in which doxologies, professions of faith, and prayers abound, that is, in which the subject realizes himself or herself according to the various requirements of faith. Therefore the use of the first person is typical in religious language, even when objective facts are stated: in the "creeds" we do not find "there is one God," but, "I believe in one God."

Above all, in religious language (at least in that of the major religions, which try continually to surpass the "magic" attitude with which man wishes to secure for himself superior powers in order to obtain some advantage), it is characteristic that the self-implicative aspect has incomparable *depth*. While in everyday language, promises, congratulations, condolences, etc., refer to very limited and superficial aspects of personal life, the religious act by its very nature goes to the core of existence, which "consecrates" itself entirely to the Other. The sacrifice, such a widespread act in the various religions, expresses in a very appropriate way the radical force of religious self-implication, which goes as far as death.

The "salutary" and therefore radically "self-implicative" function of religious speech, characteristic of faith, also determines the way in which the realities belonging to the economy of salvation are described in ecclesial language. This is very different from the way in which philosophy describes the same realities.[8]

The ideal of most philosophies is to formulate an absolutely objective definition, in which the person speaking almost disappears, and both the object and the subject are ideally considered in a neutral way, so that the existential commitment of the knower has no influence on cognition. The ideal of religious description, on the other hand, is to speak to us in such a way that each of us may be subjectively changed. The more that knowledge unites the knower with the subject itself, the more this can be obtained. Therefore, whereas the philosophical treatment of a subject will try to obtain an abstract concept as exact as possible, the religious proclamation, on the contrary, will aim at emphasizing the various aspects of reality in a convergent way, in order that the knower may realize its historical, individual, and unrepeatable concreteness.

The ambition of the philosopher will be to achieve a description of things in themselves, in which being appears in an aseptic way, deprived of any appeal to human subjectivity; the prophet, on the other hand, considers as more important that aspect of the reality he proclaims that touches the knower himself, which highlights his value, and which therefore also stimulates affectivity. In the philosophical image of reality, therefore, the sensible representation will be an element to be bracketed, whereas in religious contemplation it is a help to appeal through imagination to the whole dynamism of the human psyche.

The comparison we have drawn explains why the various stylistic forms of *symbolism* (allegory, parable, personification, simile, metaphor) are considered an imperfection in a metaphysical analysis, whereas religious language cannot do without them.

Religious speech must present the mystery, that is, the concrete supernatural gift. Since it is a completely different reality from the objects of sensible experience, it can be expressed only in analogical concepts; and since it is a question of a reality (and not an abstract concept), it is not possible to be content with an analogy of concepts. It is necessary to find an analogy of the realities themselves. It will therefore be necessary to use symbols, that is, images that, in the structure of their analogies, not only explain, but to a certain extent also give a glimpse, through the concrete representation, of the gift that transcends experience. Therefore the language of ecclesial life cannot renounce the use of images.

The Scholastic tradition considered this necessity a lowering of ecclesial language to the level of uncultured minds, "ut saltem vel sic rudes eam capiant, qui ad intelligibilia secundum se capienda non sunt idonei."[9] This way of thinking presupposes that poetic language, rich in symbolism, is "infirma inter omnes doctrinas." This is mistaken. Chaucer's "Whan that Aprille with his shoures sote the droghte of Marche hath perced to the rote,"[10] is certainly not an adaptation to the uneducated, incapable of appreciating a good treatise on metereology or psychology. Symbols are a way of saying what clear and distinct concepts are unable to express.

Yet, after the modernist crisis, Catholic theologians became even more loath to admit that symbols are suitable means to express the mysteries of faith. In fact, in the discussion with the modernists, the term "symbol" was interpreted as designating a purely arbitrary sign, which has no objective relationship with the reality it is desired to express, as the flag, for example, is an arbitrary symbol of a country. Characteristic in this respect is the expression in the encyclical *Pascendi*, according to which the modernists thought that the formulas of faith are "only" symbolical representations of the reality believed.[11]

Actually, however, there exist symbols that, by their very nature, are capable of expressing, of "showing," the object to which they refer. H_2O means water not only because of an arbitrary convention, but also because, given a conventional chemical system, it expresses something on the composition of water, that is, it says something more than the mere word "water." This is all the more so of images that express a way of behaving, or a role.

When we say that an individual behaves like a lion or like a mad dog, we really express something of the attitude of the personality. Thus we, too, are the image of God, since seeing us (especially the apex of mankind, Christ) we see the Father (cf. John 14:8).

We ought to study more deeply the comparison between the concept of analogy, accepted in the epistemology of Catholic theology, and that of the symbol, used particularly in Protestant theology.[12] For our purpose, however, it is sufficient to note that religious language in general, and the language of ecclesial life in particular, are characterized by the abundant use of symbols, and that it is not just a question of a superficial stylistic element, but of an essential structural element. The revealed symbols of Christianity say something about the very reality of the mysteries, which cannot always be expressed with an accumulation of concepts. This is so particularly of the symbols that refer to the "economic" aspects of the mysteries, such as that of the vine and branches, which describe in St. John the relationship existing between Christ and his disciples, and that of the body and its members, with which St. Paul expresses ecclesial communion.

The third characteristic feature of the ecclesial linguistic event is that it bears to a marked degree *the trace of the past.*

To some extent, every institutional religion is bound up with an original and a privileged religious experience, which has given it its particular nature. Dependence on the "founder," on the "sacred texts," gives nearly all religious language an archaic tone. This is particularly noticeable in Christianity. "In many and various ways God spoke of old to our fathers by the prophets; but in these last days he has spoken to us by a Son... (Heb. 1: 1–2).

It would be a mistake to suppose that the different revelations, received from Abraham's times to the end of the apostolic age, were expressed in a language extraneous to time and history. If it had been so, contemporaries would not have understood them. Therefore the sacred books use the vocabulary, the syntax, the image of the world, characteristic of nomads four thousand years ago, of the farmers of Canaan, the exiles of Babylonia, the fishermen of Galilee, the Hellenistic environments. It has always been known, of course, that the message can and must be translated into linguistic forms corresponding to the various times. In fact, the ecclesial tradition has assimilated patristic, monastic, Scholastic interpretations, etc., which mingled with what remained of the previous phraseology.

All this often seems quite normal for Catholics, raised in the cultural environment of the Church, since for us these elements belong to an atmosphere we inhale with ease. Objectively, however, the fact remains that many elements of ecclesial language are perfectly intelligible only by means of historical studies. In fact, it is not possible to eliminate from the preaching of the Church statements such as the one that the Christian "belongs to the kingdom of God, because the sacrifice of the Cross has freed him from the slavery of sin"; but kingdom, sacrifice, and slavery are, for modern people, archaic representations that have no direct empirical foundation.

In conclusion, the linguistic event, in which ecclesial life is realized, postulates an expression in which we find radical self-implication, symbolism, and lexicographic and syntactic archaism. These linguistic qualities cannot be eliminated because they correspond to the deep reality of ecclesial life itself. Therefore the language (lived and spoken) of ecclesial life is inevitably different not only from technical, scientific, or artistic language, but also from that of everyday life. It follows from this that the question, which we designated as the starting point of theology, is inevitably raised: How must the ecclesial linguistic event be interpreted?

The Predicate: The Interpretation of Ecclesial Life

The very nature of ecclesial community life calls for an interpretation.

The Necessity of an Interpretation

It is necessary, in fact, to discover the affirmations without which the self-implicative sentences do not have full intelligibility. It is not possible to commit oneself, saying: "I hope in you, Lord," without admitting that "God exists," "God is good and faithful," etc. It is necessary to explain the symbolical expressions, indicating the point of contact and the difference between the symbol and reality. It is not possible to deepen one's own affective union with Christ, the Good Shepherd and the Lamb of God, without setting oneself the problem of how two such different images can be realized in one person. The archaic phraseology must be translated into a present-day way of speaking. One could hardly participate personally in the Mass for a prolonged period without asking oneself in what sense terms such as sacrifice, altar, offering, etc., are used.

The interpretation corresponds in the first place to the rational nature of humans, who aim at understanding the reality in which we live. To wish to remain confined in the inevitable obscurity of the language of faith would be to repress the spontaneous impulse of intelligence. The interpretation is postulated, however, not only by the requirement of individuals, but also by the very life of the Church. The Church, in fact, must continually remake and develop her own liturgical cult; she must establish the operational requirements of her own faith as contingent situations vary; she must determine the limits of her own orthodoxy, indicating which doctrines can be professed while remaining in her unity, and which, on the contrary, separate one from her. Above all, the salvific mission of the Church has to proclaim the faith to those "outside." This calls not only for testimony but also for a certain translation of the message she lives, in a way that it can be understood by those who have not yet had the experience of ecclesial life.

In St. Paul's letters and in the writings of St. John, we find the formation of a theology based precisely on this line of reasoning. The same necessity, a permanent one in the history of the Church, always works at developing a theology. In fact, history does not show a spiritual revival, a reform of religious life, a pastoral renewal, the development of some Christian Church, community or sect, without a corresponding theology, suitable both for the local grass-roots experience and for the cultural background. Even when these communities had originally a clearly anti-intellectual tendency, such as Franciscanism, the Waldensian, or Catharist movement, and some spontaneous groups today, they inevitably reached, and reach, the point of constructing a theology of their own, as a new branch or an antithesis to the theology of the Church at large.

All three of these movements contained some strong strain of anti-intellectualism. Within the Franciscan community, from the first years of the order, there were those who saw the commitment to the intellectual life, academic involvement and scientific theological study as a betrayal of both the purposes of the Franciscan brotherhood and the intent of St. Francis. The Waldensians and Catharists are two sects which consider their teaching to be that of the primitive Church and thus pure and uncorrupted or uncontaminated by later theological development and elaboration. The Cathari flourished in the South of France in the twelfth century. They were known also as Albigensians. The Waldensians continue to exist in small numbers in Northern Italy.

"The interpretation," however, must not replace the original language with the scientific language characteristic of theology. Religious experience would be paralyzed if it were forced to express itself exclusively in scientific language, or if it even had to assimilate internally its structure. One of the results of the liturgical movement was the discovery that the prayers formulated with the categories suggested by Neo-Scholasticism, in spite of their doctrinal accuracy, remained sterile for religious impetus and piety. Examples of this would be certain formulas of acts of faith, hope, charity, and contrition, which though accurately expressing the formal object of these acts, did not facilitate their development at all. The return to the language of the Bible and the Fathers, on the other hand, gave a new impetus to the spiritual life of the Church.

The interpretation demands, therefore, a kind of permanent bilingualism, by means of which believers live in a way that is in conformity with the language of faith, but are able to explain their faith (to themselves and to others) also in the technical language of theology. The formula "fides quaerens intellectum" does not indicate an effort to replace one way of living Christianity with another, but expresses a bipolar dynamic structure, as a result of which the same experience must pervade simultaneously two different planes of human interiority.

The "Critical" Nature of the Interpretation

In human sciences, there exist carefully worked-out ways for the interpretation of cultural and linguistic realities. Psychology and sociology offer methods with which it is possible to set forth exactly the meaning of religious phenomena, and it is possible to check the accuracy of the explanation. For example, especially as regards the external and quantitatively measurable aspect of a religion, carefully prepared surveys can be used; the phenomena can be interpreted, analyzing them by means of the introspective collaboration of some subjects, chosen with suitable criteria. Finally, it is possible to study written documents, characteristic of religious life (songs, prayers, programmatic declarations, diaries, and literary works), thus bringing out their real meaning. Especially in the sixties, the new interest in religious psychology and sociology gave rise to a number of essays of unquestionable value in all these fields. But all this research is still very far from belonging to theology, properly speaking, even if it refers to the life of the Catholic Church and even if it is carried out by believers who go about their work in the light of faith.

The sociological and psychological method, used, for example, in the sphere of pastoral theology, is distinguished from theological method in the full sense because research carried out with the procedures of human sciences tries only to describe and explain existing reality — what exists in actual fact. Faith not only says that a salvific value is incarnate in the ecclesial community, but also teaches us that there is a gap between what exists in ecclesial life and what should exist, both because it does not yet exist (since the development of the Church has not yet reached completion), and because it no longer exists (because sin, existing also in the Church, has deviated or blocked some possible ways of historical development).

Observing only the phenomenal aspect of behavior, customs, institutions, material manifestations, and ecclesial preaching itself, it is not possible to know the forces that, according to faith, exist in the reality, that is, the degree of perfection that ecclesial life should reach (or should have reached).

In a certain sense, this gap exists in every scientific description. An examination of the present level of life on earth does not tell us with absolute certainty what levels evolution will reach in the future; analysis of any reality never gives the ideal form of the species, but only of an individual, nearly always imperfect in a certain sense. Science, however, can create a futurology, at least a conjectural one, by plotting the regularity of the previous phases of development and projecting them into the future; it can reach cognition of the ideal form, through induction, which rises from comparison of various individuals to the universal. These procedures are not at the disposal of theology, since the phenomenon of which it has empirical knowledge is not only unique individually, but is also the fruit of divine creative freedom, the decisions of which cannot be determined *a priori.*

Yet theology finds in its very object indications that not only permit, but also demand that the scientific analysis of ecclesial reality should go beyond the reality of the existing fact, and judge it by comparing it with a reality that out to be. In this sense, the theological interpretation of the community life of the Church is not purely descriptive, but is "critical," since it finds, precisely in its object, the necessity and the criterion to compare what is with what, according to the internal postulate of the reality, ought to be.

The theological interpretation is "critical" because it emphasizes those properties of the ecclesial phenomenon by which one is certain that God guarantees its substantial validity. This task of interpretation belongs to fundamental theology. But the "critical" nature of theological interpretation shows up also in dogmatic theology. It must distinguish what is genuine and authentic in ecclesial experience and what, on the contrary, is the fruit of misunderstanding, abuse, and confusion. Its task is to discern the inalienable "substance" of the Christian message from the various contingent "forms" in which it is incarnated in the succession of various cultures.

Theological research, therefore, can only partly be compared with that process through which religious ethnology describes Islamism, Buddhism, etc. The point of contact lies in the fact that both religious ethnology and theology aim at a description and interpretation of a religious structure. But although religious ethnology, which prescinds from the validity of its object, can only describe phenomena, theology can also judge them, since it finds the criterion to discern the authenticity of its single elements in ecclesial experience itself, accepted through faith.

Critical interpretation has two aspects: it implies, on the one hand, a return to the *past*, in which revelation was accepted once and for all, and progressively understood by the Church; and is, on the other hand, an *opening-up to new experiences*, which emerge in every era of history and appeal for a renewal and rethinking of the ecclesial reality.

In theology, the critical interpretation of ecclesial life is obtained, in the first place, through a comparison of present day experience with *documents coming from the past* (Scriptures, creeds, and other testimony, in which the faith of preceding centuries is expressed). In fact, the faith with which theologians accepts the ecclesial phenomenon prevents their interpretation of Christianity from being limited only to a description of the existing phenomenon.

Theologians, as believers, accept the intrinsic postulate in the phenomenon described by them, according to which the whole of present ecclesial life is a substantially legitimate development of divine revelation, contained in Scripture and set forth in the past preaching of the Church. In other words, theologians admit as a postulate of this faith that present ecclesial life can and must be interpreted in continual comparison with the Scriptures, as they have been and are understood in the Church.[13]

Reflecting, for example, on the cult of the saints, theologians will record not only the way in which this cult is lived and understood in the Church today, but, in the very practice itself and in community consciousness, they will find an appeal to Scripture, to the works of the Fathers, and to the teaching of the Magisterium. In these documents theologians will seek not only justification of the essential elements of the present behavior of the Church, but also the criteria that will enable them to correct and complete it.

Of course, judgment on the present in the light of the past will not signify that everything that is in conformity with the past is good, while everything that differs from it is wrong. Such archaeolatry (which has sometimes cropped up in the history of the Church, as, for example, in Jansenism) does not take into account the historicity of revelation and its transmission. It is necessary to recall the possibility of a legitimate development of ecclesial life and teaching.[14] It is possible that the documents of the past are difficult from the present reality because points of view now appreciated had not yet been considered.

Furthermore, the word of God is never expressed in a pure form; it is always incarnate in the language of some culture. Therefore, it is possible that some aspects of past positions are due not to the faith, but to the image of the world and to a culture in which the faith was expressed. But the more that the assertions of past preaching appeal to an interpretation of the word of God, the more that they have been confirmed by the charismatic life they have called forth and, above all, the more the Church has considered them with its teaching authority as inseparable from the way to salvation, then the more the voice of the ecclesial past becomes a norm to judge present-day ecclesial life.

Thus we can see that taking ecclesial experience as the starting point of theology does not detract in any way from the importance of biblical studies, the testimony of the Fathers, or the further history of dogma, which Vatican Council II declared to be essential for theological formation.[15]

A second aspect of the critical interpretation of ecclesial life lies in the opening of this life to *ever new historical situations*. Christ, sending his Apostles to make all peoples disciples, and promising to remain with them to the end of time (cf. Matt: 28:20), did not confine himself to the past or to a given cultural area, but is the Pantokrator, the universal Lord who is yet to come (cf. Rev. 1:8).

The believer, accepting present-day ecclesial life as a development of God's word, which is substantially valid but always perfectible, believes that this word can be expressed in any cultural complex of the present and of the future, and can give any new human situation a meaning in the horizon of salvation. Christian truth can always be expressed in various civilizations by means of the representative schemata and the concepts belonging to that civilization; and to every new historical, physiological, psychological, and social condition there can always be applied both the certainty that God cooperates in it for the good of those who love him (cf. Rom. 8:28), and the questions, inseparable from faith, "What shall I do, Lord?" (Acts 22:10). Accepting this conviction, we are merely recognizing that the word of

God is addressed to all living at all times, and in all places, and is therefore valid for them.

The critical interpretation of the linguistic event that is the life of the Church today is carried out completely, therefore, only when the ecclesial existence of today, interpreted and corrected with the help of the documents of the past, is also projected toward the ever new cultural situations that occur in history. This happens through continual "transconceptualization": the expressive, creative, and affirmative contents are conceived and uttered in the framework of the conceptual structure and image of the world as it is today.

Furthermore, theology turns to new situations when it interprets and judges the signs of the times in the light of the Gospels: the new (existing and existential) events that challenge ecclesial conscience are compared with the total image of the economy of salvation, to discover their meaning, and to determine the behavior that the Christian must assume with regard to them.

Consideration for the present situation, therefore, must not be deemed a pastoral corollary, extraneous to the scientific study of dogmatic theology, even if (especially in the cultural area of Neo-Scholastic theology), people are accustomed to think in this way. In the past, in fact, a historical mentality made the vast majority of dogmaticians think that real theological reflection takes place in a world of universal ideas, outside the flux of historicity. Biblical, patristic, and conciliar testimonies were translated into a language that was considered perennial, universal, rooted in human nature itself, regulated by the laws of "common sense," or of a prescientific and universal grammar and logic. The facts and theories of the day had to be compared with the message expressed in this language.

It is now accepted that a universal and perennial language does not exist, either in the spoken language or in the structure of thought. There exist only the various cultures, each with its language, although there is, of course, a sufficient structural analogy between these cultures for the human mind to be capable of knowing history, that is, to be able to interpret one culture by means of the other. In any case, that language that was considered universal and perennial (that of Scholasticism) is seen now as a particular language of the clergy, used between the two Vatican Councils. Today it is reserved to a very few specialists.

The Church urges that beginning with the teaching of dogmatic theology in seminaries, students should "learn to seek the solution of human problems in the light of revelation, to apply its eternal truths to the changing conditions of human affairs, and to express them in language which people of the modern world will understand."[16] This is not a work that comes after the interpretation of the sources; rather it is in this application that one finds the interpretation.

The critical interpretation of present-day ecclesial life, made by means of a comparison with the documents that emerge from the past and by means of the opening to ever new situations, cannot be conceived, therefore, as three successive steps, but as the convergence of three simultaneous dimensions of a complex cultural reality. While we read the Gospels, today's questions reecho in our minds and, vice versa, we look at present reality in the light of the Gospels. Therefore, all the requirements of the critical interpretation of ecclesial experience are operating in the whole of theology, and the various branches of theology are nothing but aspects of this interpretation, carried out from different points of view, and therefore with different methods.

The starting point of theology is, therefore, a question in which theologians, realizing the community reality of the Church, ask themselves what are the affirmations, conceptually exact and systematically arranged, through which ecclesial life is expressed, explained, and judged, in the light of the Scriptures commented on ecclesially, in view of the present cultural situation.

The assertions of which we are speaking, do not all, of course, concern the Church and her life. Some refer to God, to Christ, to the ways of salvation, and above all to us, who need to be saved and who find salvation in Christ. The question, which constitutes the starting point of theology, wishes to explain ecclesial life, but this life can be explained only by knowing the whole economy of salvation, willed and revealed by God.

CHAPTER NOTES

1. Cf. Paul VI's address to the International Theology Congress, in 1966: AAS 58 (1966-II), pp. 892–93. The interpretation of the Lutheran H. Geisser, *Die Funktion der Theologie in Kirche und Gesellschaft nach der Deutung Paulus VI*, in: Neuenzeit, Greinacher, Lengsfeld, *Die Funktion der Theologie in Kirche and Gesellschaft* (Munich, 1969), p. 110–28, which shows only one aspect of the complex pontifical doctrine, distorts its meaning.

2. C. Molari, *La fede e il suo linguaggio* (Assisi, 1972), p. 116.

3. W. Kasper, *Methods of Dogmatic Theology* (Shannon, 1969).

4. M. Schmaus, *Catholic Dogma*, trans. by A. Laeuchli (New York, 1968).

5. The ability of language to transmit not only schemata but also mental contents is a result of the psychological function of symbols: cf. C.G. Jung, *Psychological Types* (Princeton, N.J., 1971).

6. M.D. Chenu, *La théologie est-elle une science?* (Paris, 1957), pp. 53–4.

7. The division comes from K. Buhler, *Sprachtheorie, Die Darstellungsfunktion der Sprache* (Jena, 1934), and is developed by further linguistic analysis in J. Ladriere, *L'articulation du sens* (Paris, 1970).

8. On this subject, cf. the important pages of Y. Congar, "Le moment 'economique' et le moment 'ontologique' dans la "sacra doctrina,' " in: *Mélanges offerts à M.D. Chenu* (Paris, 1967), pp. 135–87; an application of this distinction to the theology of St. Thomas and of Luther is found in O.H. Pesch, *Theologie der Rechtfertigung bei Martin Luther und Thomas von Aquin* (Mainz, 1967), pp. 935–48.

9. St. Thomas, *S. Th.* I, q.1, a.9

10. The *Canterbury Tales*, Prol.

11. "Philosopho certum est, repraesentationes obiecti fidei esse *tantum* symbolicas" not cited in DS, is reported in Denzinger-Bannwart 2087.

12. Some indications can already be found, e.g., in C. Journet, "Sur Mircea Eliade et l'histoire des religions," in: *Nova et vetera* 30 (1955), pp. 305–18; H. Looff, *Der Symbolbegriff in der neueren Religionsphilosophie* (Köln, 1955), G.B. Mondin, *Il problema del linguaggio teologico dalle origini ad oggi* (Brescia, 1971) 333–87; E.L. Mascall, *Existence and Analogy* (London, 1949); *Words and Images: A study in the possibility of religious discourse* (London, 1957).

13. For the doctrine on the relationship between ecclesiastical teaching and Sacred Scripture, cf. W. Kasper, *The Method of Dogmatic Theology* (Shannon, 1969).

14. Cf. J. H. Newman, *The Development of Christian Doctrine*; B.J.F. Lonergan, *Method in Theology* (London, 1972); W.R. Fey, *Faith and Doubt* (Shepherdstown, 1976).

15. Cf. *Optatam totius*, n. 16.

16. *Optatam totius*, n. 16.

3

Recourse to the Past

It is characteristic of theology to have recourse to the "sacred texts" coming from the past. A line of reasoning, even if it concerns religious problems, is not considered "theological" if it disregards Sacred Scripture, ecclesial tradition, and the doctrinal position of the hierarchy. The problem is in how this recourse is integrated in the view of theology, conceived as an interpretation of ecclesial life; that is: What is the meaning and what must be the nature of the question the theologians put to these historical documents?

The matter is at present a deeply felt one. In our times, geared to the future, it is difficult to admit that the preceding phases of historical development can contain the keys to present problems. Careful reflection has been carried out, particularly in the study of the concept of "truth" in the Bible and in discussion of the meaning of the "infallibility" of the ecclesiastical Magisterium.[1]

These discussions alone, however, show the intrinsic difficulty of solving our problem. In fact, to the question, why do we try to understand the meaning of the life of the Church today by studying the ancient texts, the spontaneous answer would be that these texts contain the truth, eternal and immutable. But, although we all use the adjective "true" in everyday life, no sooner do we begin to penetrate its meaning speculatively than we meet with a multitude of explanations.[2]

Is truth a correspondence between the subjective mind and objective reality? Or the self-manifestation of things? Or a consistency of knowledge with the structure of the intellect? Or a way of thinking adapted to the development of life? Or what proves to be correct empirically?

It cannot be seen with what right the theologian can opt for one of the definitions of truth (and therefore, for one of the philosophies of knowledge), before he or she has even established the meaning of an inquiry, especially since the terms *emeth* or even *alètheia*, which are mainly translated with the word *truth*, have a different meaning from

all these concepts.[3] That explains why excellent theological epis-
temologies, although they seek the path toward truth, not only do not
speak of this concept, but also mostly allude to it only in remarks
scattered here and there.[4] It is therefore indispensable to discover the
meaning of recourse to the past by starting from within ecclesial existence itself; that, by asking in what sense the reliance of the authority
of given texts belongs to the *authenticity* of ecclesial life, and to what
extent the *reasonableness* of this life implies the noetic validity of the
texts.[5]

Let us gather here those characteristics of the "recourse to the
past" that explain the methodological behavior postulated by the
situation of theology today.[6]

The Meaning of Recourse to the Past

Right from the beginning of the organization of theological science, mention is made of the "auctoritates," that is, biblical, patristic,
magisterial affirmations that have a normative function, in a certain
sense, to direct the understanding of faith.

It is now a commonplace that recourse to the Bible, to tradition,
and to the Magisterium cannot consist in an indiscriminate use of affirmations isolated from their original context and exploited in favor
of later doctrines.[8] In the same way it is taken for granted that recourse to the authority of the teaching of the past does not aim at re-
storing a "theology of the past," since the message of hagiographers,
of the Fathers and Masters of the faith becomes fully intelligible to us
when it is read against the background of the questions of the present. Yet there is no theology without the attitude of "listening" to the
message that emerges from the Scriptures, from the works of the
Fathers, and from the documents of the Magisterium. The fundamental validity of this behavior is based on two principles.

The first is *the indefectibility of the Church*. The Church, in fact,
considers herself the depository of divine promises, according to
which, in spite of human frailty, there remains and prevails in her the
eternal presence of Christ, who communicates his Spirit and thus
guides the Church in believing and in preaching the gospel.[9] On the
basis of these promises, the Church believes that the universality of
the faithful "cannot err in matters of belief," and "clings without fail
to the faith."[10]

The second principle is that the Church, through history, *has ac-*

cepted certain texts as authentic expressions of her faith because they
were composed (in different ways) under the influence of the Holy
Spirit. Ecclesial reflection distinguishes various types of this influence, using the terms "inspiration," "illumination," "assistance." In
spite of the essential difference in the depth and extension of the action of the Holy Spirit, the indefectibility of the Church is bound up
with the validity of these texts. The presence of the Holy Spirit in the
Church would have been suffocated if the books accepted in the biblical canon had not been inspired and if the great options with which
throughout her history the Church solved controversies concerning
the genuine meaning of the Bible and the way in which the Scriptures were to be applied to the questions of the various ages, had
been contrary to the postulates of the message of salvation. The indefectibility of the Church and the historical fact that the Church links
up membership in her unity of salvation with agreement with certain
assertions (in the "dogmas") determines, therefore, *the value of these
assertions.* According to Father Schillebeeckx, "if the responsible
ecclesiastical officials in the collegial union did not enjoy charismatic
assistance necessary to formulate the faith in circumstances that require it, in a correct, legitimate, and faithful way, which is, therefore,
binding on all the faithful (albeit always in a context that is conditioned historically), the divine promise of the permanence of the
Church in truth would be a vain and negligible *flatus vocis.*"[11] If the
documents accepted by the Church were *once* binding with regard to
salvation, they can never become negligible for the theologian, who
seeks the understanding of faith.

In fact the validity of the dogmas formulated successively
throughout the history of the Church depended not merely on subjective (and therefore changeable) factors, but on the fact that they indicated the way through which the individual members of the community of salvation could find the correct relationship with the Father.
This way is Christ, who once and for all became present in human
history as Savior,[12] once and for all was manifested as such to mankind through the testimony of the Apostles, and prolonged up to the
present in ecclesial preaching.

Certainly, it must be taken into account that all these texts, even
inspired or defined ones, speak a human language and therefore do
not express completely even just a particular aspect of reality. In fact,
they do not even express it with absolute faithfulness. Between every
human assertion and the mystery of God, the difference is always
greater than the conformity.[13] It is also true that when a reality

changes, an assertion can lose its conformity with it. The proposition, "the Pope is called Pius," once true, became false at a certain moment of words, valid assertions may become invalid: the sentences "the Word Incarnate has only one physis," or "man lost free will through sin," once orthodox, have become heterodox in today's terminology. But if admitting given assertions once constituted a condition for being in the right relationship with the order of salvation, it is an unchangeable and eternal fact that, in that existential situation and in that linguistic context, they authentically expressed an aspect of reality. In this sense (and only in this sense) those sentences remain necessarily normative forever for ecclesial thought.

The propositions thought and uttered under the influence of the Holy Spirit, though they do not imprison the mystery within themselves, remain valid, in fact, as arrows indicating the way toward correct understanding of the mystery (and toward a correct understanding of reality in the light of the mystery). Throughout history, the arrows are multiplied, and their convergence helps us to an ever deeper theological understanding. Knowing how the reality of salvation had to be thought of in a certain number of existential and linguistic contexts, makes it easier for us to find formulas of expression that fit in with our own present context. It must also be said that what is contradictory to one of the formulas definitively recognized as valid, in that meaning and in that context in which they were accepted, can never become an authentic expression of ecclesial life.

It follows that to formulate our faith it is not necessary to determine empirically which formulas stimulate theological life in the community (a control that in practice would be impossible). It is true that the valid formula always fosters life, but a formula is not valid because it has this efficacy in fact (for psychological, sociological reasons, etc.), but it is efficacious since it is in noetic continuity with that "deposit" that "handed over" to the Church "once and for all," which can be ascertained with recourse, studies methodologically, the biblical, patristic, and magisterial "auctoritates" of the past.

"Phenomenological" Nature of Recourse to the Past

In a preceding phase of theology, Scripture, the liturgy, the works of the Fathers, and the decisions of the Magisterium, were considered mainly (if not exclusively) as *noetic principles* of theological study. It was supposed that the various documents, at least as a whole, were easily intelligible, especially in the light of the Magisterium; in any case, any problems of interpretation could be solved by the auxiliary sciences (by exegetics, by the history of dogma, etc.). It was thought that real theological work consisted in *reasoning on the content* of the sources, pointing out the logical tie between the sources and the present teaching of the Church. Theological research, therefore, mainly answered the question whether a given affirmation was true, since it was already known and at least implicitly taught by Scripture, the Fathers, etc. This way of thinking was the fruit of a theology that was mainly polemical, which envisaged as adversaries first the Protestants and then the modernists. The purpose of reflection was to defend a "thesis" (the present teaching of the Church), showing how it belonged to the "deposit" of revealed truth, always identical throughout the centuries.

Some twenty years ago, the "return to the sources" brought about a change in the approach of theology. The observation that Rahner made with regard to research on the history of penance applies to the whole of theology. Historians of dogma now "will no longer have to prove in the first place that the Fathers "also" said and lived what the Church teaches and lives today. But they will have to investigate, with more leisure and loving study of patristic doctrine, what the Fathers have to tell us about penance, in addition to the truths that are clearly and exactly present in the theological conscience of today. Historians will try to make the patristic doctrine a ferment for dogmatic progress and a stimulus to discern more clearly something new, which the ancients already saw and knew...."[14]

A maturing of perspective is not arbitrary, but corresponds to a postulate of history.

Works written on religious language today often stress that at present the objection of those who refuse to believe in the dogmas of the Church is no longer the negation of given assertions (God created the world, in God there are three persons, Jesus Christ is present in the Eucharist), but rather the affirmation that these assertions do not have any meaning. The temptation that threatens the theologian is the one expressed incisively, for example, by D. Antiseri: "We in theology work solely with pseudoconcepts: with words and other linguistic entities completely deprived of meaning...."[15]

The bewilderment with regard to the meaning of the various dogmas has a certain parallel with that felt by the philosophers before metaphysical affirmations, without which it is not possible to construct a philosophy. "At a certain point, we have the sensation of no longer understanding and, in fact, of misunderstanding even the little that we think we understand ...."[16] Philosophy tries to overcome the obstacle by taking refuge in a description of the objective image of phenomena, which puts in brackets any affirmation not based on this analysis. The "phenomenological" method, so widespread in philosophy today, is precisely "an effort to learn, through empirical events and facts, essences, or ideal meanings that are grasped directly by intuition through particular examples, studied in a detailed and concrete way."[17] "Phenomenology is the search for authenticity, and its importance in contemporary philosophy would not be understood unless by starting from the embarrassment of incomprehension and from a widespread sensation of the inauthentic ...."[18]

The same tendency to emerge from the crisis through descriptive analysis, freed from every *a priori*, is common to all sciences today. This is the meaning of Heidegger's often-quoted sentence: "The authentic movement of sciences takes place in the revision of their fundamental concepts, a revision more or less radical and self-explanatory. The level of a science is measured by the extent to which it is capable of handling the crisis of its fundamental concepts."[19] Here, too, the phenomenological nature is unmistakable; it is not the fundamental axioms, assertions, or theses that are the object of revision, but the concepts.

It is inevitable that a similar orientation should be observed in theology. The question most emphasized in the search for the understanding of faith is not the one *an sit* (whether certain assertions are true of not), but rather the one *quid* sit (that is, what is the meaning of the linguistic event that constitutes our life in the Church?).

It is clear that in theology the two questions cannot be completely separated. Since we believe that ecclesial life, understood as a linguistic element, is valid, we admit that the doctrine postulated and implicitly contained in it is true. However, for the sake of methodological precision, it is necessary to distinguish the descriptive task from that of assertion, and lay more stress on the first aspect, in consideration of the present sensibility of thought.

On the one hand the phenomenological approach allows theological research to constitute a connatural and necessary explication of ecclesial life rather than remain on its fringes.[20] On the other hand, this methodological trend integrates theology into the pluralistic and essentially "antidogmatic" whole of modern sciences. Theology, in fact, since it presupposes faith, is a connatural development of it and therefore corresponds to an existential postulate of it. Since it is a scientific explanation of the rationality and the meaning of faith, it corresponds to a question that is legitimate even for an atheist: What do those who live the religious experience in its Catholic form believe, and why do they believe it?

The phenomenological approach already makes sufficient appearance in the whole conception of theology, as a result of which the science of faith becomes in the first place an interpreter of ecclesial life. But this methodological conception is manifested far more in the way in which recourse is had to the documents of the past in this critical interpretation.

In the numerous historical monographs that, as a result of Leo XIII's invitation, were dedicated to the interpretation of St. Thomas, we can often observe the passing from the question about what St. Thomas thought on a given subject, to the question of how things stand in themselves. This passing from exploration of the thought of a subject to that of the structure of an object, is not legitimate, even if it is believed that the thought studied is true, that is, in conformity with the reality.

In fact, the method with which one describes the phenomenon thought by an author, and the one with which one affirms that the phenomenon thought corresponds to reality, are too different to be used indiscriminately. Today, therefore, one of the indispensable rules for theological research into the documents of the ecclesial past is to raise the problem very clearly as to whether one wishes to interpret a source or whether, on the contrary, one intends to prove an assertion. Even in biblical theology itself it is necessary to distinguish propositions that refer to the message of an author from those that affirm something about God, about the person, about the world, that is, directly about reality itself.

It is one thing to establish that according to St. Paul justification is obtained only through faith and baptism; it is another thing to search whether in actual fact faith and baptism are always necessary for reconciliation with God. It is one thing to note that according to St. Augustine children are guilty of a sin inherited from Adam and therefore doomed to hell if they are not baptized; it is another thing to affirm that in actual fact all unbaptized children go to hell. Therefore the first recommendation that the director of a dissertation of a historical character makes to a theology student is not to force the thought of the author he is preparing to study by introducing into it affirmations that he should have made.

In order that the description of previous stages will not be af-

fected by later ones, a clear division is observed in theological literature today between the descriptive part regarding the thought of
others and the constructive part in which the attempt is made to solve
a problem in the light of faith. In view of the difference in the techniques of thought necessary in both parts, a monograph deals mainly
with only one of these tasks, leaving it to the collective consciousness
of the Church to integrate the specialized research into the synthesis
of the understanding of faith. In fact, it is not infrequently proposed to
divide the teaching of theology right from the beginning according to
the various specializations, entrusting to the exegete, the patristic
scholar, the liturgist, the historian, the student of dogmatics, etc., the
treatment of the same subject at various levels.

In this division of tasks, the specific function of the dogmatician
would be to use the results of expository studies, working out in this
way an interpretation of the mystery that, while remaining in continuity with the preaching of the past, will correspond to present mental requirements. This may be right, provided, however, that the various teachers live in such a communion of thought that the student
will not only acquire a file of detached information, but will also discover the organic unity of the connecting thought. In fact, the study of
previous phases of dogmatic development in theology has the function of *supplying models of thought with the help of which we, too,
will be able to find our way of professing the same dogma.*

The continual tension between the necessity of remaining faithful
to past teaching and that of living our faith in dialogue with contemporary thought has the result that students must neither cancel from
their minds the categories and questions of the present nor introduce
them through an "exegesis" into the reading of the sources. These
two opposite but essential requirements highlight the importance of
hermeneutics in dogmatic study today.

Hermeneutical Nature of Recourse to the Past

In our theology schools, especially in the cultural areas not influenced by Romanticism, the procedure of explaining the texts of the
past by appealing to the "regulae recte loquendi" was widespread for
a certain time. Exasperating some principles of a medieval logic of
language, people tended to suppose that human nature postulates the
same linguistic structure in all peoples and in all times: to each essence there corresponds a concept, to the concept a word; syntax is an

objectivization of the law as of thought, which in their turn reflect those of objective reality.

In this perspective, the phenomenological interpretation of a formula consisted only in the grammatical and logical analysis of its use. It is known what applications this conception found in some Neo-Scholastic manuals in the explanation of the sentence "this is my body" (from which, it was claimed, the dogma of transubstantiation could be proved through deductive reasoning), or in the explanation of the sentence "you go to eternal fire" (a premise from which the existence of a real, and not a metaphorical, fire in hell could likewise be deduced).

This phenomenon has often been described and criticized; in fact, most theologians today were formed in this intellectual context and feel its deficiency acutely. We must not, however, exaggerate the scope of this criticism, as if it were valid against the Catholic theology of all periods. As a matter of fact, this critical oversimplification, through which the explanation of the texts was restricted to a grammatical and logical analysis, is an episodic deficiency of the end of the nineteenth century and the beginning of the twentieth century, which can also be explained as an antimodernistic stiffening, while the great theological tradition always stressed the necessity of a deeper interpretation.

As is known, the main literary type of theological research was, for fifteen centuries, the biblical and patristic "commentary," in which hermeneutics, that is, the technique of interpreting, had already a considerable development. To begin with, it was the divergencies met with in the Bible that called attention to the necessity of establishing the rules of the art of interpreting Holy Scripture.[21] In the Middle Ages, the more abundant and almost juridical use of patristic "auctoritates" made further reflection on the hermeneutical problem necessary, with the intention of solving the discrepancy between the various "sentences."[22]

In recent centuries, the use of these proceedings became more necessary and more radical since it was essential to take a position in the conflict between the image of the world that ecclesial preaching was tied to, and the one that the sciences were gradually constructing. In fact, to avoid the absurdity of two truths, it was necessary to clarify what was the "real meaning" of the dogmas of the Church.[23] It is known how this problem gradually also invaded the historical level and is manifested in a new view of the development of dogma[24] and in the approach to ecumenical dialogue.[25] All of that developed in the general context of culture. The hermeneutics of the Fathers owed a great deal to the Rabbinic and Hellenistic interpretative art.[26] From the Middle Ages to the beginning of this century it was jurisprudence that exercised the deepest influence on the technique of scriptural and patristic interpretation. At present, it is philosophy, partly through the mediation of Protestant theology, that opens up new horizons for reflection, inducing the theologians to rethink their categories.

When the unquestionable novelty of hermeneutical concern (a branch cultivated more intensely by present-day theology)[27] is thus set in its frame of reference, it will no longer seem a disconcerting break with the past, but rather a new form corresponding to a perennial requirement, made more urgent today in the science of the faith. It is very important, in fact, for the theologian to protect himself or herself from two opposite reactions: one is to ignore hermeneutics, considering it "the art of making a text say the opposite of its content"; the other is the irrational use of a pseudohermeneutics that seeks to preserve the traditional ecclesiastical formulas without giving them, however, any meaning that meets with the favor of fashionable ideologies.

There are three *principles that govern the hermeneutical procedure,* without which the theologian of today cannot validly have recourse to the documents of the past.

The first one is that a text coming from another cultural context cannot be read as if it were produced in the language of one's own environment, but rather it must always be interpreted. This necessity results from the *anthropological* discovery of the diachronic and synchronous diversity of various structural cultures. The influence of different cultures on man's way of reasoning strengthens the *epistemological* concept that denies the possibility of a clear separation between "objective content" and "subjective forms," stressing the fact that all human cognition is always a response to a previous question, takes its place in an existing dialogue, and therefore has a meaning only in a given historical context.

Therefore, the interpretation cannot aim at freeing a doctrine from all historical, personal, and community conditioning (which is impossible), but tries to recognize subjective categories as such, and to express the message of the sources in its own historical, personal, and community categories.[28] The universal necessity of interpretation has long been recognized as valid for the reading of the Bible. We can find confirmation of it in the canonical prohibition to publish translations of the Bible in modern languages without notes. Only in recent times, however, has the principle been extended not only to the writings of the Fathers, but also to the documents of the Magisterium.[29]

The *second principle* is that, generally speaking, every text can be "interpreted"; that is, the content of every text can also be understood and expressed in other cultural languages. It is true that we can never exhaust all the fine shades of individual interiority in a communication that, by its very nature, uses intersubjective signs, that is, signs that are not absolutely individual; no one doubts, however, that normal, cultivated persons can substantially explain their experiences to others. This possibility must be extended also to statements made beyond the spatial and temporal frontiers of the various cultural cycles.

In fact, no one denies on principle the possibility that the works of Plato, the code of Hammurabi, the sayings of Confucius, can be understood and judged. The same applies to biblical revelation and the explanation it received throughout the centuries in ecclesial preaching, far more deeply studied and far nearer to us in the unity of Christian religious experience. We admit that a full interpretation of the message of salvation is possible only thanks to grace, since it requires that the listeners should put themselves fully at the disposal of the word of God. To understand this word truly is to accept it, and it is accepted in *metanoia,* in conversion. But here we are speaking of an interpretation that arrives at the written word through participation in ecclesial life, and therefore within the sphere of grace.

The *third principle* refers to the subject of "recourse to the past" for theological hermeneutics. Since it is a question of writings spread over nearly four thousand years, in extremely different cultural cycles, belonging to a very wide range of literary types, corresponding to aims that are not only affirmative and expressive, but also creative of community life, the interpretation of these texts requires the use of various techniques, and is carried out in differentiated research and publications. No individual person can master such a complex array of equipment.

Therefore the real subject of theological hermeneutics is the community. The various publications inform a "collective consciousness," stored in libraries, made accessible through reports on research, bibliographical guides, etc. Individuals use the objectivizations of this collective research to the extent to which the solution of their problems makes it necessary. Therefore, the new theology implies essentially not only acquired concepts, but also the art of using critically the results of others' research as working tools and that of putting one's own research at the disposal of others, so that the research can be judged, used, and surpassed.

In view of the complexity of the procedures used in the interpretation of an ancient text, it is useful to distinguish the *various stages* of hermeneutical work.

It can be considered a prior condition to obtain an authentic, not corrupt, text, having recourse, when possible, to critical editions. If a translation is used, it is necessary to check if it is judged accurate by competent persons; at least in the crucial points of the interpretation it is desirable to have recourse to the text in the original language.

In the real and proper work of interpretation it is opportune to distinguish a philological, a historical, and a dogmatic level.

The philological exposition consists of the determination of as much of the meaning of the text in its "literal" reality as is possible with references to the text alone. It requires in the first place *lexicographic* analysis on the basis of general semantics and the concrete context of the sentence. It is known that many misunderstandings arose, for example, from failure to realize that in the works of St. Augustine the word "nature" does not designate a reality adequately distinguished from grace, and the term "freedom" does not mean an active indeterminateness.

Also the determination of the syntax of sentences, which we overlook so easily in the fast reading to which the tempo of modern life accustoms us, is part of philological analysis. The subject of the sentences ending with the predicate "anathema sit," for example, is not a false proposition (as is said so often), but a person who accepts a doctrine by which he puts himself and others in danger of breaking with the unity of faith, and is therefore excluded from the community of salvation. This is decisive in determining with what certainly the proposition in question must be declared "false."[30] The relationship of the various sentences in the text as a whole also becomes clearer when, for example, the conjunctions (coordinating or subordinating) that integrate the sentences into the structure of the discourse are considered.

It is worth stressing the conjuctions that introduce the various paragraphs in the declaration of Vatican Council II on "human activity as infected by sin."[31] The words "vero," "tamen," "enim" (ed. Dehoniana, n. 1436), "enim," (*ibid.*, 1434), "quapropter" (*ibid.*, 1435), "ergo" (*ibid.*, 1436), make the articulation of the text transparent, and taking them into account we can discover the "argumentative" dynamics of the text, which gathers the premises and the consequences of the statement "human progress brings with it a strong temptation" (*ibid.,* 1433). Also in the chapter on "a new earth and new heaven,"[32] the conjunctions "quidem" and "sed" (ed. Dehoniana, 1439), "sane," "tamen," "licet," (*ibid.,* n. 1440), "enim," "tamen" (*ibid.,* 1441) show that the text is trying to harmonize two opposite tendencies, and taking this antithetical structure into account, we can avoid absolutizing an aspect or proclaiming as a message of the Council a concession made to a complementary point of view.

The *second level* of interpretation is the historical one. Its object is no longer the text considered just in its impersonal reality, but the meaning that the author wished to express, that is, the *"communicative intention."*

A written text always keeps, in fact, the fundamental structure of language, and therefore presupposes one subject addressing another; without a minimum of intersubjective relationship, language would lose all meaning. Therefore, after one has understood the grammatical meaning of a text, the first question that one must ask oneself is: In what sense does the author appeal to my agreement, what does the author wish to tell me, what was the "communicative intention," which may be didactic, creative, or expressive, according to the prevalence of one of the functions of language?

The communicative intention is really known to the extent to which one reconstructs the consciousness of the person speaking, with the speaker's other convictions, appreciations, and motivations, through which the interpellating meaning of his or her expression becomes intelligible. Such a reconstruction implies knowledge of the historical context, both diachronic (since the communication takes its place in a development of successive facts) and synchronous (since there is a stand with regard to a complex contemporary situation).

The meaning of a sentence in a particular case can only be known on the basis of knowledge of the historical situation in which it was uttered. In a theological text, "historical content" means (a) functional context (if it is a question of an address delivered by a bishop to persuade the people, or by a scholastic philosopher to refute his adversary), (b) ideal context (the error or vice that is challenged), (c) personal context (character and style of the author). It is a question of discovering, through history, the author's "vital form," as a result of which the linguistic event becomes comprehensible in a new way.[33]

In religious language (which is the language not only of Scripture, but also of the documents of the ecclesiastical Magisterium), the "historical" aspect is particularly important. The main purpose of a prophet, an evangelist, a bishop, is not to enrich the intellect with new knowledge, but to make the community live fully the life of Christ. The communicative intention of the authors in the first place is to call upon people to act, speak, and think in the way that, in the present situation, is postulated as the way of salvation. Therefore, though admitting that certain situations are permanent because they are inseparable from the community of salvation, consideration of the historical context is far more important in the interpretation of theological sources than in, for example, the hermeneutics of philosophical texts. It follows from this that a theological research that applies the sources immediately to present problems, neglecting historical analysis (e.g., wishing to obtain from Exodus a theology of liberation), is only superficially current. In reality it is an essentialist theology put in the service of uncontrolled ideologies.

Finally, there is a *third level* of interpretation that, presupposing the historical one, goes beyond it and discovers a perennially normative value in the communication made. We call it the "dogmatic" hermeneutical level.

The surpassing of the purely historical level in the interpretation of theological sources is postulated by the fact that they contain divine testimony incarnated through human speech, the value of which is connected with that of human interpellation, but not limited to it. The surplus value given by divine testimony to the human word becomes intelligible if we reflect on a principle that present-day theology likes to express by quoting a sentence from St. Thomas, "actus credentis non terminatur ad enuntiabile, sed ad rem."[34] God, in fact, by giving valid norms for our behavior, reveals something about reality itself. Christian revelation does not call upon us to take into account events that happened once and for all.

This true cognition continues to challenge us and becomes a norm, in the light of which we can solve other problems not belonging to the immediate historical context of the source. For example, the narration of the agony of Christ in the garden was originally intended for purposes very different from that of testifying to Christ's full humanity, not absorbed in divinity.[35] However, the actual narration also reveals this reality, and therefore gave valid norms for the later Church to take up position on the problems of Docetism, Monophysitism, and Monothelitism.[36]

The same transcendence of the message as compared with its historical horizon can also be noted by showing that the various historical contexts are not watertight compartments, but have a certain internal communication. For example, the teachings on the saving value of faith and works in Rom. 3:28 and in Gal. 2:14 are located within different semantic horizons. Both, however, have points of contact with our situation, so we can compose universally valid formulations precisely by taking into account the complementary difference of the two contexts and their analogy with ours.

It is clear, however, that the passing-from historical testimony to a norm that is also valid for us must be tested critically. It is necessary to determine in what sense and for what reason an appeal set in a historical framework constitutes a word of God addressed to everybody, to myself. It is in this verification that the opening toward the categories and the problems of the contemporary cultural context takes place.

We must repeat, in fact, that these two aspects of the one theological task (interrogation of the past and opening to the present) are not two successive phases of the research, as if it were possible in a first phase to compare present-day life with the documents of the past, and in a second phase to project the result on the screen of the mental forms and problems of today. Interpretation is carried out when, in one act, the message conceived in formulas handed down from the past is expressed in others corresponding to the present cultural and existential context.

CHAPTER NOTES

1. For the discussions caused by H. Küng's book, *Infallible?* (Garden City, 1971), cf. the bibliographical list in H. Küng (ed.) *Fehlbar? Eine Bilanz* (Einsiedeln, 1973) pp. 515–24.

2. A. Carlini's article, "Verità," in: *Enciclopedia Filosofica* (ed. 2) 4, pp. 878–90, with its abundant bibliography, can give an idea of the complexity of the problem mentioned here: also "Truth" in W. Brugger, K. Baker, *Philosophical Dictionary*, pp. 427–439.

3. Cf. I. de la Potterie, "De sensu vocis Emeth in Vetere Testamento," in: *Verbum Domini* 27 (1949), pp. 336–54; 28 (1950), pp. 29–42; Quell, Kittel, Bultman, "Alètheia," in *Grande Lessico del Nuovo Testamento* 1, pp. 625–74; A.C. Thiselton, "Truth" in *Dictionary of New Testament Theology* 3, pp. 874–902; J.L. McKenzie, *Dictionary of the Bible*, pp. 901–02.

4. Cf., e.g., the place of reflection on truth in B. Lonergan, *Method in Theology* (New

York, 1972) chap.12–13, and E. Simons, K. Hecker, *Theologisches Verstehen, Philosophische Prolegomena zu einer theologischen Hermeneutik* (Düsseldorf, 1969).

5. From this analysis, with a reductive method, it will be possible to arrive at a theologically justified conception of "truth," which will be the one set forth by E. Schillebeeckx, *Revelation and Theology* (New York, 1967), illustrated philosophically in L. Pareyson, *Verità e interpretazione* (Milan, 1971). However, this analysis goes beyond the limits of our Introduction.

6. For a more systematic treatment of the theories briefly indicated here, cf. E. Schillebeeckx, *Revelation and Theology* (New York, 1967).

7. Cf. M.D. Chenu, *La théologie au douzième siècle* (Paris, 1957); pp. 351–65; Y. Congar, "Norms of Christian Allegiance and Identity in the History of the Church," in: *Concilium* 83 (1973), pp. 11–26.

8. For the development of use of the Scriptures in dogmatic research, cf. J. Beumer, *Die theologische Methode,* in: Schmaus, Grillmeier, Scheffczyk, *Hanbuch der Dogmengeschichte* I/6 (Freiburg, 1972), pp. 126–36; on the correct use of the declarations of the Magisterium, Y. Congar, *Situation et tâches présentes de la théologie* (Paris 1967), pp. 111–33.

9. Cf. Matt. 28:20; John 14; 16–18; 1 Tim. 3:15.

10. *Lumen gentium,* n. 12, Vatican Council II, *The Dogmatic Constitution on the Church,* (November 21, 1964).

11. E. Schillebeeckx, *The Problem of the Infallibility of the Church* in: *Concilium* 83 (1973), pp. 77–94.

12. We are thinking of the stress laid on the "hapax" of the paschal mystery in Heb. 9: 12–28.

13. Cf. the sentence of the IV Lateran Council, "inter creatorem et Creaturam non potest similitudo notari, quin inter eos maior sit dissimilitudo notanda" (DS 806). Therefore, the revealed truth can never be exhausted in a human formula (AAS 42, 1950, 568), and the knowlege of it can always increase (*Dei Verbum,* n. 8). This matter is studied more deeply in two documents of the International Theological Commission and of the Congregation for the Doctrine of the Faith, in 1973: cf. the commentary of M. Flick, "Chiesa permissiva o Chiesa repressiva," in: *La Civiltà Cattolica* 124 (1973) III, pp. 455–66.

14. K. Rahner, *La Penitenza della Chiesa* (Roma, 1968), p. 524; *Forgotten Truths Concerning the Sacrament of Penance;* in: *Theological Investigations* Vol. II (Baltimore, 1963), pp. 135–74.

15. D. Antiseri, *Filosofia analitica e semantica del linguaggio religioso* (Brescia, 1969), p. :, p. 27.

16. P. Filiasi Carcano, *La metodologia nel rinnovarsi del pensiero contemporaneo* (Naples, no publication date) p. 29.

17. A. Lalande, *Dizionario critico di filosofia,* It. trans. (Milan, 1971), p. 300.

18. P. Filiasi Carcano, *op. cit.*, p. 30.

19. M. Heidegger, *Being and Time* (New York, 1962).

20. We think that in this point is found the justification of the program of studies mentioned by R. Voillaume, *La vie religieuse dans le monde actuel* (Ottawa, 1970) pp. 54–55.

21. An example is found in Augustine, *De doctrina christiana*, 1. 3, *PL* 34, 65–90.

22. Cf. for example the famous work of Abelard, *Sic et non*, *PL* 178, 1339–1610.

23. Cf. this concern as early as Vatican Council I (DS 3017), which led, in recent times, for example, to the new positions with regard to evolutionism.

24. Cf. the characteristic principle expressed in *Gaudium et spes*, n. 62.

25. Cf. *Unitatis redintegratio*, no. 17, Vatican Council II, Decree on Ecumenism, (November 21, 1964).

26. For the classical inheritance, cf. the text of Boethius, *In Porphyrium dial.* 1, *PL* 64, 9; for the Judaic one, J. Danielou, "Hermeneutique Judeo-Chretienne," *in: Vari, Ermeneutica e tradizione* (Rome, 1963), pp. 225–62.

27. A comprehensive presentation of this phenomenon is found in: R. Marle, *Introduction to Hermeneutics* (New York, 1967); C. Geffre, *New Age in Theology*, (New York, 1974).

28. On these theories (which are, of course, only mentioned here) cf. J. Cobb, *A New Hermeneutic* (New York, 1964); B. Mondin, *Il problema del linguaggio teologico dalle originia ad oggi* (Brescia, 1971) pp. 461–80 (an exposition of Gadamer's thought, with useful bibliographical indications) and pp. 480–95 (a summary of Ricoeur's theory).

29. Cf. the Instruction "Mysterium Ecclesiae," June 24, 1973. On the deep meaning of this necessity, cf. the observations of P. Ricoeur, *Finitude et culpabilitè: 2, Le symbolique du mal* (Paris, 1960), p. 326.

30. Cf. Y. Congar, *Situation et tâches présentes de la théologia* (Paris, 1967); *Tradition and traditions* (London, 1966).

31. *Gaudium et spes*, n. 37.

32. *Gaudium et spes*, n. 39.

33. Behind this consideration lies the concept of "linguistic game," on which the philosophy of language has reached deep results, very stimulating for theology, the theological implications of which are not yet fully elaborated. Df., e.g., K. Lorenz, *Elemente der Sprachkritik, eine Alternative zum Dogmatismus und Skeptizismus in der analytischen Philosophie* (Frankfurt, 1970); W.P. de Pater, *Theologische Sprachlogik* (Munich, 1971), pp. 160–77.

34. *S. Th.*, II–II, q. 1, a. 2, ad 2.

35. Cf. P. Benoit, *The Passion and Resurrection of Jesus Christ* (New York, 1969).

36. For a definition of the terms see: K. Rahner, H. Vorgrimler, *Theological Dictionary*, pp. 131, 293, 294; *The Oxford Dictionary of the Christian Church*, pp. 413, 931, 932.

4

Opening to New Situations

The task of theology is to deepen the understanding of faith for the people who must live it today. Theologians cannot help having recourse to past ecclesial life, from which every new theology that really remains such emerges, and by which it is nourished. They must also be concerned in making Christ's eternal message palatable to the people of today. In fact, if Sacred Scripture read in the Church is, according to an expression coined by Leo XIII[1] and utilized by Vatican Council II,[2] "the *soul* of theology," this already tells us that it is not *all* theology in itself, but needs a "body" in which to become incarnate. This "body" consists of the form of thought, the mentality, and the set of problems peculiar to that environment in which the word of God must be read, proclaimed, and applied.

The impact of past teaching on today's thought is felt in various ways, through various channels. To study the complementary variety of aspects and of channels through which the eternal Word becomes incarnate in the culture and the language of the people of today, it is useful to begin by analyzing the phenomenon of the so-called *theologies with the genitive.* The multiplication of writings presented as a theology *of* some author, *of* some environment, *of* some mystery, *of* some empirical reality, is a characteristic of our times.

This use (even if it has sometimes had aberrant manifestations) can, in the last analysis, be connected with the New Testament, which designates the Gospel not only as the word of God, of the Lord, or of Christ, but also as the word of truth (e.g., 2 Cor. 6–7; Eph. 1:13; Col. 1:5; 2 Tim. 2:15), and of grace (e.g., Acts 14:3), the word of the Cross (1 Cor. 1:18), the word of reconciliation (2 Cor. 5:19) and of life (1 John 1:1; Eph. 5:26). The various terms, through referring to the same message, are not completely interchangeable because they designate different aspects of the message, each of which can be developed in theology in its own way. When contemporary theology exploits this possibility, distinguishing various theologies with a series of genitives, it highlights, above all, the many ways in which the word of God is confronted with the cultural and existential situation of the environment. By distinguishing the various models in the use of the genitive, let us try to circumscribe some aspects of the theological opening toward the present.

The Genitive of Origin

The first example in the use of genitives appeared in those works that multiplied at the beginning of the twentieth century, that took as their subject the theology of some thinker of the past: the theology of Tertullian,[3] of Cyprian,[4] and even of St. Paul.[5] Apparently, these works have nothing in common with the present situation, since they have in mind an exclusively historical purpose. Yet it was just in this way that the attention of a whole theological generation was called to the possibility, not to say the necessity, of this opening. In fact, by trying to "decipher" the message of an author who lived many centuries ago, it was discovered that the "code" to make the thought intelligible is merely the existential, cultural, and linguistic context of a given age, to which the author belonged.

Those historical works caused, in their time, a kind of scandal: was the theology of St. Paul different from ours? The answer was that the same system of truth can be conceived and expressed in various cultural and linguistic systems. Interpretation of the thought of the past proceeded, in fact, by continual detachment from the forms of modern thought, since it was constantly necessary to remind the reader that not only did a term or a formula not mean what it means today, but also that the questions the ancients endeavored to answer were very different from ours, and that the premises considered certain, from which the reasoning of an author of antiquity set out, or which were tacitly presupposed in it, might very often seem unintelligible and questionable to the modern reader.

Thus, in historical interpretation itself, people perceived the possible plurality of contexts in which the same faith can be thought, and were attracted by the idea of constructing a theology intelligible to the faithful of today, formed in another intellectual environment. This attraction, in the stormy times of the struggle between modernists and traditionalists, could not be followed on a large scale, but it constitutes the main task of contemporary theology.

We have reminded the reader of these works in positive theology because they indicate the way by which the student can arrive at forming a theological reasoning that is at once updated and reliable.

In fact, it is often suggested that the only possible source of reading in the existential and cultural situation of the Christian today is found in popular reviews and booklets that concentrate on applying Christian doctrine, and on the behavior and intellectual life of a person living in a secularized environment.

On the other hand, in programs of study, the student of theology is called to attend courses on exegesis, patristics, liturgy, and dogma, which, in their inevitable schematic and specialized brevity, easily give the impression of presenting a crystallized doctrine, formulated definitively. Experience shows that the integration of this reading and these courses in an organic theological culture is threatened by two diametrically opposed dangers. Scylla is constituted by rejection of the traditional doctrine, which may even be considered useless junk. Charybdis is a misunderstood estimate of some historical formulation, the value of which is sometimes absolutized, as if the search for further formulations were useless, in fact almost sacrilegious.

Integration is obtained when all theological disciplines are considered in the context of the evolution of dogma. This is envisaged also in the often-quoted enumeration of theological disciplines made by Vatican Council II,[6] according to which knowledge of the earlier phases of development is understood as the seed of later formulations. The presentation of the past, a presentation open to the future, is naturally the first task of the positive disciplines. But even in systematic theology itself and, in fact, in the critical reading of present-day theological literature, it is always necessary to call to mind again the historically conditioned context of the sources, to which recourse is had in order to be able to judge in what sense they constitute a valid norm for thought today.

Therefore, the student will always have to be guided in setting each witness quoted (biblical, liturgical, patristic, magisterial) in the framework of the time that produced it. For this purpose, in private study, even of systematic theology, one must have recourse continually to basic reference works,[7] which should be kept at the disposal of everyone in the library of every seminary. Only in this way will that consciousness of the historicity of the sources be acquired, which makes it possible to transcend the past, without denying it.

The Genitive of Subject

In contemporary theological literature, the genitive is frequently used to indicate the category of persons who *promote* a given theological movement, or to whom a given theological movement is particularly addressed. Thus the desire is expressed for a theology of the laity, written by and intended for the laity which will be different from that of ecclesiastics; or for a theology *of the industrial age*, thought out by persons living in this environment and suitable for them. Those who are in touch with the Third World know how often the particular churches postulate a theology for themselves, affirming the necessity of a theology of *Latin Americans, of Asians, and of Africans*. It is clear that these genitives forcefully stress an opening onto present-day situations in which theology developed.

As happens so often with apparently unprecedented novelties, more careful reflection shows that this movement can be linked with quite traditional precedents. When St. Paul notes that "Jews demand signs and Greeks seek wisdom," and preaches Christ crucified as the power of God for the former and as the wisdom of God for the latter (1 Cor. 1:22–25), he states a theology of the Jews and a theology of the Greeks, since he uses the categories of two cultural environments and goes beyond them, showing their insufficiency, while applying them to the paschal mystery.

In the post-Apostolic Church, a distinction is made between the theology of Judeo-Christians and that of Hellenists.[8] Similar differences existed also in later centuries. It is significant to compare two works, both composed to lead a catechumen of Hellenistic formation to embrace Christianity: the *Protreptikos* of Clement of Alexandria, and the *Mystagogical Catecheses* of Cyril of Jerusalem. The first work is the theology of a "didascalos," who concentrates on the individual growth in intellectual conviction; the other is the theology of a bishop, who stresses the sacramental aspect of Christian regeneration. Medieval theology was already aware of the difference existing between the theology of monks and that of Scholastics,[9] between the theology of the Dominicans and that of the Franciscans.[10] In the light of these historical facts, it is easy to understand why the theology of the people of today, though remaining within the boundaries of the same faith, need not necessarily be identical with that of our ancestors, and why a legitimate pluralism can exist in contemporary theology.

It was once thought that the difference between the various traditional theological schools (e.g., Scotist, Thomist, Suarezian) lay mainly in some particular theses, admitted by some and rejected by others. Deeper studies have shown that the conflicting particular theses are nothing but a marginal manifestation of the different ways in which even the same doctrines were understood.

The way one understands the faith is influenced by various factors. Let us indicate some, by way of example, that are easily found in the history of medieval theology.

In the first place, the temperament, that is, the psychological make-up of the thinker, influenced also by one's national and social origin, is important. It is no mere chance that the problem of the "disinterested" nature of pure love was never raised by Greek and Latin thinkers, but became almost an obsession for certain theologians coming from the same environment in which people were avidly reading the romances of the court of King Arthur and the poetry of the "dolce stil nuovo" (Abelard, St. Bernard, Richard of St. Victor, Aelred de Rieval).

Another factor is the previous experience of the person undertaking the study of theology. For example, we have on the one hand, an intense religious experience, nourished by biblical symbolism and reflectively analyzed and, on the other hand, a knowledge of dialectics or, even more, of the "libri naturales" of the Greeks and Arabs, which are difficult to integrate into the Christian view of the world. These give theological thought a different direction right from the beginning. The tension between monastic theology and Scholastic theology can be explained, in no small way, by taking this factor into consideration.

Of course, the form of thought is characterized also by the techniques through which reflection is carried out, which in their turn are determined by the institutional framework. The fact that, in certain monasteries, works of the Greek Fathers existed in a good Latin translation, that their reading was fostered by the whole rhythm of life of the community, and their integration promoted by the abbot's short, daily homily, or that some were obliged to take part in highly specialized discussions on problems not solely connected with the necessities of a Christian affective life, leaves, of course, a deep mark on their respective theologies.

The purpose to which intellectual activity is more or less consciously geared is also incisive. This can already be seen in the diversity of the normal medieval university functions, when and where the "magister sacrae paginae" himself set forth the same problem, in a slightly different way, in a biblical comment, in a debate, and in a sermon in church.[11] The difference was far deeper, however, when an end or a finality gave a direction to the whole of life. The thirst for contemplation in the disciples of St. Anselm, or the zeal to preach in the mendicant orders, or the desire to know in intellectuals of the type of John of Salisbury, evidently changes the whole structure of thought.

The influence of the subject's life-style on the nature of one's theology becomes even clearer if we recall that today many historians indicate as the root of the difference between Catholic and Protestant theology not the admission or denial some objective assertion, but the prevalence of a subjective, methodological attitude, such as the preintelligence of the person, the "sapiential" or "prophetic" nature of the discussion, or the biblical or ecclesial approach to the research. This subjective difference causes a prereflective total perspective, as a result of which even propositions of identical content are understood differently, and as a result of which it becomes psychologically understandable why mistakes will be made with greater probability in a determined direction rather than in another, and why persons who think starting from different personal prescientific approaches almost inevitably arrive even at contradictory affirmations from time to time.

All the difference so diligently highlighted by historians may seem slight compared not only with the ones encountered among contemporaries of Pius X and Paul VI, but also with the ones that divide newcomers to theology from the generation of their teachers. Therefore it is not absurd to think that the theology of those who are formed in the present social and cultural background will be different from that of their teachers, even if the latter, from the doctrinal point of view, are not "preconciliar."

The renewal of theology, which took place during and after the Council, consists mainly of an attempt to adapt the Christian message to the contemporary outlook. This implies in the first place the tendency to express the great intuitions of faith with concepts akin to contemporary thought. For example, there is a characteristic tendency to describe theological life no longer with the metaphysical categories of habit, act, quality, but with categories taken from the life of the person, from dialogue-meeting, from community life. This effort also appears in the attempt to separate the message of salvation from an outdated image of the world, and to express it (though without yielding to the temptation of concordism), in continuity with the image of the world that is accepted today. We are thinking, for example, of the projection of the dogma of creation or of the original sin on the background of the evolutionary conception of the universe, of the living, and of humanity.

The tendency to adaptation is also revealed in the pastoral and not assertive style deliberately chosen by the Council, and in the attitude with which it preferred to "use the medicine of mercy rather than of severity" and "to meet the needs of today by showing the validity of its doctrines rather than by renewing condemnations."[12] This style is not limited only to the way of communicating ideas, but also expresses an inner attitude of the theologian, who integrates the ecclesial message in the world dialogue, through which mankind is seeking the solution to its problems.

It would be a mistake, however, to think that renewal is made once and for all. In the twenty years following the Council, the rhythm of change has become ever more rapid. It is significant that the Italian Episcopal Conference, giving guidelines and norms for the preparation of future priests, feels the necessity of beginning with the description of present-day problems and recalls them just at the beginning of the directives for intellectual formation.[13] Psychological characteristics (community sense, awareness of one's own personality, psychic instability), basic experiences (e.g., the struggle for liberation), fundamental cultural direction (such as psychological and sociological interest), intellectual techniques preferred (group research), an image of the world (the evolutionary conception of the universe), characteristic purpose or end (to dialogue rather than convince), cause the prospects of the theology of tomorrow to be very different from that of yesterday and even from that of today.

It is an important and almost agonizing question that is raised by every student of theology (and also for every teacher), namely, how it is possible to continue the Incarnation of the Word, in the existential and cultural forms of the environment.

In the first place, an important condition is to "be suitably involved in normal human activities," the necessity of which is recognized in the documents of the hierarchy today.[14]

Another indispensable condition is a wide cultural formation, which goes beyond the almost exclusively classical formation that was once considered, especially in Latin countries, suitable for the clerical world. It is significant that a well-known presentation of present-day theology begins with the description of art, literature, human sciences, and philosophy in our century.[15] The path of an *aggiornamento* of theology will have to proceed in this perspective, taking care, however, that the study of present-day culture always remains a way of engaging in theology (in continuity with the present cultural situation), and does not become the definitive and principal subject of study, replacing the theological interest.

Very often it will be of great help in updating one's thoughts to read the great contemporary theologians, who have already made a synthesis of the revealed Word and the forms of contemporary thought. The reason why there is so much interest in Catholic countries today in the study of Protestant theologians is precisely that Protestant theology preceded Catholic theology by almost a century in opening up to modern culture, often going to the other extreme, that is, losing continuity with the sources. Here, too, it is necessary to ensure the organic integration of readings in a valid structure of thought. It is completely harmful to read booklets or articles written in a doctrinal system not well known to the reader, before he or she has reflected on the fundamental lines of the synthesis these readings should serve and in which they must be judged. This is particularly important as regards reading translations from foreign languages, coming from cultural backgrounds that are different.

For example, the book by Helmut Thielicke on the fear of the student of Lutheran theology to accept the office of pastor, is given in the Italian the title: *Perplessità del seminarista di fronte al ministero sacerdotale*[16] (*The Seminarian's Perplexity Before the Priestly Ministry*). This puts the reader on the wrong track because it makes him forget that the students with whom the work deals have never lived in a seminary and do not believe at all that the pastor is more of a "priest" than other believers. To avoid misunderstandings, it is very useful to begin reading with an overall presentation of the thoughts of the individual theologian, which helps to integrate single opinions in that doctrinal system outside which they often have no meaning.

The normal way of cultural updating is the use of theology, studied during the usual academic curriculum, in the pastoral ministry, in which experience on the one hand deepens theory (showing how it answers questions that are actually deeply felt), and on the other hand reveals the way to communicate the doctrine in forms suited to the requirements of the community. From time to time priests, engaged in pastoral work, are heard to say that what they learned in the seminary is of no use to them in the apostolate. It is correct to say that the doctrine is of no use to them in the form in which they learned it. But it often happens that they do not realize that they could not have utilized their experience and later reading if a foundation had not been laid through the systematic study of theology. This foundation sustains the subsequent superstructures, even if it is no longer visible. In fact, only those who have really assimilated the basic teachings are able to move easily into catechetic and homiletic exposition of the Christian message. Others merely repeat sentences, taken either from the classical manuals or from the repertory of a newspaper pseudotheology.

The Genitive of Object

The most frequent use of the genitive to specify how a given theology leads to new existential and cultural situations, refers to an object to which a work or a movement gives special attention.

The polarization of theological study on a given object may have various degrees of depth. A rather superficial form gathers the statements on a given subject that are found in ecclesial preaching. Examples of this type of specialization are the classical theological treatises or, to give a more recent example, the various theologies of work. A more penetrating variant of concentration on an object aims at interpreting the *whole* Christian message in terms of a given concept, in such a way that the whole message becomes the background of a question, and in every assertion of faith note is taken of what concerns the question that holds the theologian's attention. This is the way in which the "theology of man" proceeds, following the "anthropological turning point" inaugurated by Rahner, or the "political theology" as J. B. Metz understands it.

There is a third way of understanding how theology must face a given reality, that is, the one in which the approach chosen is declared the only valid one. This denies the legitimacy of theology not concentrated on that object. We think that this is true of those traditional theologians who accept as the only genuinely theological point of view the one *sub ratione deitatis.* The "theology of the cross," as understood by Luther, also proceeds in this way. Not only does he wish to stress that the whole message of salvation receives a meaning in the light of Christ's Cross, but also he rejects as an idolatrous distortion any "theology of glory" that aims at getting to know what is invisible in God, through visible creation.

Here we prescind from the question of the degree of concentration of any "theology of something." We are concerned with the *diversity of meanings,* in which an object can polarize theology. In fact, it is precisely the diversity of meanings that is important for the possible variety in the ways that theology can lead to concrete situations. In the analysis of the meaning, we think it is possible to distinguish three typical forms: the theological interpretation of religious realities; the religious interpretation of profane realities; the profane interpretation of religious realities.[17]

The Theological Interpretation of Religious Realities

It often happens that a given aspect of Christian life, at a certain moment of history, takes on special importance. Believers, who need to reflect intellectually on this specific aspect of their own Christian experience, see that systematic theology does not dedicate much space to the object of their interest. These are moments when there flourish studies that set forth and arrange the revealed doctrine in relation to the interpretation of a given aspect of ecclesial life. That may happen with regard to a concept,[18] with regard to a biblical theme difficult to assimilate in the theological system,[19] with regard to an ecclesial function,[20] or a form of the Christian ideal.[21]

By giving single religious realities a theological interpretation, the life of the Church becomes more conscious. Theology also benefits from this service it renders to ecclesial praxis, since its relationship with lived reality becomes more intense. Also a new point of view helps to bring out of their isolation the elements that make up the traditional systematic framework of theology and thus enrich them. For example, reflection on the Mystical Body contributed a great deal to the birth of a more dogmatic ecclesiology, and studies on the themes of the religion of Israel prepared the renewal of theology against the background of the history of salvation.

Right from the beginning of their studies, students of theology can complement the usual theological treatises with a theological interpretation of religious realities. With the help of a theological dictionary,[22] they can reconstruct and deepen the meaning of the religious terms used in the lessons or in the manuals. In this way, they will relate the content of the various theological disciplines with one another and with the reality of ecclesial life.

The Religious Interpretation of Profane Realities

If by the term "profane reality" we intend to designate what is not connected in any way with the Absolute, or what is fully intelligible regardless of this connection, the dogma of creation teaches us that there is nothing profane in the universe. Using, nevertheless, the distinction between religious and profane, we give these terms a different meaning; that is, we refer to the way in which the various realities manifest to the human mind their unconditional connection with God. For example, the realities made by us to concretize our relations with God are almost "transparent," since (in a given cultural context) they manifest their transcendent meaning at once: such are the objects of worship, rites, stories regarding the divinity, and prayers. Other realities are so connected with the core of human existence that a person open to the supernatural easily and spontaneously divines a religious sense in them, and therefore they are surrounded by the institutionalized halo of the "sacred" in nearly all great cultures. Examples of this are birth, the initiation of adults, marriage, struggle, and death. There are, on the contrary, other realities that could be called "opaque" because they do not manifest, at first sight, what their relationship with God is. It is necessary to break through the outer layer of their immanence to discover their definitive and sacred meaning, and to determine how they are integrated in an image of the world, determined by faith.

In a culture permeated by religion, in which the very institutional structures suggest a religious interpretation of the whole environment, the number of profane realities may be limited to new items, which are not yet assimilated by the faith of the community. In a secularized culture, where institutions wish to be nonreligious or lay, and where, therefore, individuals must find the transcendent meaning of their world, the number of profane realities grows continually. Yet Christians especially, called to imbue their whole life with faith (Cf. 1 Cor. 10:31; Col. 3:17), cannot renounce discovering how God judges the various phenomena that emerge from the flux of history, and therefore, what is the behavior that must be adopted with regard to them. This search (that is, "the religious interpretation of profane reality") is the task of theology.

In this context one understands the explosion of the most active branch of present-day theology: the theology of the world (the theology of earthly realities, of history, of secularization, of development, of progress, of revolution, of peace, of liberation, or whatever may be the name of the various movements belonging to this trend). A bibliography, published by the World Council of Churches, records more than two thousand publications dedicated to these subjects since the end of World War II.[23] There are some who interpret this literary eruption as a phenomenon of the disintegration of theology, which, having lost interest in God, is in search of another subject. This is a simplistic interpretation, or at least one that cannot be generalized.

In every new situation, Christians inevitably ask themselves and the community in which they live: "Brethren, what shall we do?" (Acts 2:37). That is, what is the behavior that our faith demands in this situation? The question, predominately an ethical one, necessarily implies a dogmatic one: how does God judge this situation? What is the providential meaning of that "visit of God" that takes place invisibly in every change of human existence? What is the intention of the Creator when he puts given realities in my path?[24] Of course not only external events, but also the very aspirations of mankind, being realized in our moment in history, must be judged in the light of the divine will. "The interpretation of the signs of the times," made in the light of the Gospel, which is one of the characteristic thrusts of the Council,[25] and which, according to the directives of the Council, can no longer be absent from the teaching of systematic theology, consists precisely in this.[26]

In the present situation, the technical revolution has changed enormously not only the environment in which we live, but also, in a certain way, human reality itself. It could almost be said that we have built ourselves a new world, a new body a new soul. On the other hand, an organized Christian society no longer exists, and Christians who live in a Diaspora must interpret by themselves the new world that is coming into being and that is becoming more and more opaque as regards its religious interpretations.

The sources do not know, of course, the new realities that are arising around us, and it would be contrary to the rules of sound hermeneutics to seek in them a judgment on urbanism, industrialization, and ecology. It would be, for example, an improper extrapolation to apply the Old Testament oracles on the occupation of Palestine by Israel to express a judgment on the war between Israelis and Arabs. Theology must therefore create new ways of proceeding to find a Christian perspective with regard to the new human reality. The method will consist in comparing the contingent reality with the overall image of God's work for the salvation of the world, and to understand, through this comparison, what God thinks about the new world. In this connection we proceed on the basis of what he said regarding the world as it once was because he has not said anything about the new one. The overall objective image does not add any detail to revelation, but neither is it the result of a sum of revealed assertions. It does not contain quantitatively more data, but presents a whole that is qualitatively different from their sum, as a melody is different from the sum of the single notes, as a poem transcends the sum of the single words, and as a meeting with a person is qualitatively different from possessing all the person's personal and biographical data. For this reason the global image of God's work of salvation allows us to discover the analogy between some problems of the past and our present problems, thus guiding us to find solutions for our religious problems by analogy with the revealed solutions of the religious problems of the past.

The noetic procedure is similar to the one by which, in daily life, we guess how a friend we know intimately will react to new situations. But while the forecast of the human attitude mostly remains only probable (because the behavior of a human person, which is complex and unstable, may change), knowledge of what ancient theologians called "mores divini"[27] can arrive at a degree of certainty because God, who reveals his intimacy to his friends, always remains faithful to himself in his infinite simplicity.

However, even the human effort to "guess" divine thought on new situations always remains exposed to error. In the first place, the image of the contingent situation, which is compared with the revealed datum, is not obtained from theological sources, and therefore its validity is equal to the validity of the sociological, historical, and psychological procedures through which it has been worked out. Theologians, in fact the very documents of the Magisterium, should always imply, in their religious interpretations of profane realities, a hypothetical clause. For example, "If the phenomenon or urbanism is as you describe it and does not also have other advantages or disadvantages you have not enumerated, in the light of faith we must say that. . . ." This is very important to prevent theology from being unconsciously enslaved to an ideology.[28]

Comparing the contingent datum (the image of the new situation empirically known) with the revealed datum (the objective image of the economy of salvation), we must not hastily draw conclusions from one assertion only, but we must specify exactly the meaning of our theological affirmations, taking into account other complementary revealed truths. In fact, it is a mistake to think that an assertion regarding God's action "is not taken seriously" unless stress is laid on it to the extent of eclipsing or even denying the other truths that specify and possibly relativize its significance. For example, from God's satisfaction regarding creation ("very good"), it does not follow that sinful man can enjoy every created reality without danger to his salvation. From the necessity of reaching a certain human development in order to live as Christians, it does not follow that any degree or any form of development is always favorable to Christian conversion.

All that raises important requirements with regard to the opening of theology to new situations.

In the first place, it must be said clearly that the question, what does the faith say about the new phenomena of human history of which revelation does not speak, is a legitimate one, and a theologian who believes in revelation as the word of life, given once and for all to all people, cannot fail to take an interest in it.

It must be added, however, that faith is not given to promote, correct, or complete the empirical search for technical solutions of immanent problems. The theologian, therefore, must respect the autonomy of human sciences and must not trespass on their field in the hope of obtaining from faith concrete directives for political or social action. In this connection it is important to recall the admonition of the Council to laity, who ought not to think that their pastors are such experts in human affairs that "to every problem which arises, however complicated, they can readily give them a concrete solution, or even that such is their mission."[29]

It is also important to note that theology offers a religious interpretation of profane phenomena, since it compares the latter with what God has done (as event and as the result of these events). Therefore, a theology of earthly realities can explain the "functional" relations between the Christian and the world only if its statements are "entitatively" based on the revealed view of reality itself.

The Profane Interpretation of Religious Realities

A third way in which theology opens on to the new situations of mankind constitutes a distortion of the theology of the world, since it puts Christian theology in the service of the "world," understood in John's meaning of the word. We mentioned this temptation in another context, showing how a theological anthropology can degenerate into an anthropologized theology in which religious assertions are listened to only to the extent to which they serve as guiding principles to construct personal human existence or the future of mankind.[30]

The profane interpretation of religious realities is mostly the effect of frustration. The theologian has the impression that the world has changed. In the centuries of faith, the main and most deeply felt question of mankind was, how to be able to find the transcendental salvation offered to men by a merciful God. At present, the fundamental question is, how to be able to construct a better immanent world, in solidarity with others. The theologians go so far as to think that the only way to get Christianity accepted is to present it in its function with regard to the construction of the world in solidarity.

In this way, they are led to interpret the realities described by the Christian message solely as symbols of human advancement. A typical example of this interpretation is the use of the concept of salvation. Setting out from the fact that Christian salvation is a liberation that is not only eschatological, but already anticipated, to some extent, on earth, they promise only an immanent salvation. Under the pretext that the concept of Christian salvation must not be personalized, they abstain from proclaiming liberation from sin, death, and alienation (the root of which taken as a whole is sin), and stress only the reaction against poverty and oppression. Sin becomes a symbolical expression to indicate everything that hinders humans in their full personal and community development. The Savior becomes the one who, with his own influence (example, teaching, stimulating personality), gave an irreversible impetus to the great movement of human liberation.

To some, in this way the crisis of evangelization in the present-day world is easily solved. One can continue to repeat: "Blessed are the poor," on the understanding that Christianity ends their poverty on earth; one can celebrate the Eucharist as an effective sign of human solidarity; one can assume the role of priest, attributing to him the function of animator of the community on its way toward a more beautiful immanent future. Christianity becomes acceptable, since it justifies the absolutizing of an ideology that enjoys sympathy. But while saving ecclesiastical institutions (the formulas, rites, organizational structures), the spirit of Christianity is betrayed (the necessity of a conversion by which one abandons an immanent and selfish purpose of existence, and gives oneself up in full obedience and trust to the hidden God, who redeems us through the Cross).

This operation of "saving" Christianity does not really save anything. In fact, on the one hand, humans without the miracle of supernatural conversion, yesterday as today, are always "earthly" and "carnal"; on the other hand, religious structures are too unsuitable a covering for an ideology of collective and immanent selfishness for them ever to be accepted in a lasting way. But what is important to note from the theological point of view is that such an expression of Christianity keeps the linguistic forms of the proclamation, but neglects what, according to the sources, is the heart of all ecclesial life, that is, the personal relationship with God, in faith, hope, and charity.

This is a distortion similar to other distortions made in the past in the opposite direction: e.g., the one that made the Christian message an instrument to justify and therefore preserve social structures of privilege, stressing the Christian value of resignation of the oppressed, or which absolutized in almost an idolatrous way certain external frameworks of Christian life, such as the privileges of the clergy, sacred rites, and some theological formulas that were defended as absolutely immutable, while ignoring their function as an instrument in relation to the supernatural mystery.

The error in this approach is to accept the fundamental option of the world, masking it with the institutional structures of Christianity.

The fault in approaching theology in this way is evident if we compare it with St. Paul's preaching in Athens. The Apostle accepted an opening in the axiological system of the environment, giving it a Christian answer: the God that the Athenians worship without knowing him is the Father of Christ (Acts 17:23). In the continuity of this acceptance of their position, there is also a break, however, since Paul declares that the concrete way of worshipping the unknown God was tolerable only in "times of ignorance" (Acts 17:30), whereas now this worship must emerge from the anonymity in which it was possible for it to coexist with other forms of worship, and it must be addressed solely to the Father of Christ, who raised him from the dead and made him the judge of all men (Acts 17:31).

The profane interpretation of religious reality resembles rather the procedure of Aaron (Exod. 32:1–6). In a moment of collective frustration ("as for this man Moses, the man who brought us up out of the land of Egypt, we do not know what has become of him" — (Exod. 32:1), he declares the identity of the golden calf constructed by the people with the God who saved Israel from Egypt. In this way he introduces idolatry into the structures of the religion of Yahweh, sacrificing its monotheistic essence.

Chapter Notes

1. Enc. *Providentissimus Deus*, in: *ASS* 26 (1893–94), p. 283. The documents of the Holy See from 1909 on are found in the *Acta Apostolicae Sedis* (AAS). From 1865 to 1908 this collection was entitled *Acta Sanctae Sedis* (ASS)

2. *Optatam totius*, n. 16.

3. A. D'Ales, *La théologie de Tertullien* (Paris, 1905).

4. A. D'Ales, *La théologie de Saint Cyprien* (Paris, 1906).

5. F. Prat, *The Theology of St. Paul* (Westminster, 1926).

6. *Optatam totius*, n. 16.

7. See chap. 7.

8. Cf. J. Danielou, *The Theology of Jewish Christianity* (Chicago, 1964); Etudes d'exégèse judeo-chrétienne (Paris, 1966); *Gospel message and Hellenistic Culture,* with postscript by J. A. Baker (Philadelphia, 1973).

9. Cf. J. Leclercq, *L'amour des lettres et le désir de Dieu* (Paris, 1957) pp. 179–218; M. Mayr, *Die theologische Methode des Gerhoch von Reichersberg (Rome, 1973); D. Knowles with D. Obolenski, The Christian Century,* Vol. 2 (London, 1969); D. Knowles, *The Evolution of Medieval Thought* (London, 1962).

10. Cf. in this connection M. D. Chenu, *Toward Understanding Saint Thomas,* with bibliographical additions by A. M. Landry and D. Hughes (Chicago, 1964) and J. G. Bourgerol, *Introduction à l'étude de St. Bonaventure* (Tournai, 1961).

11. Cf. Pietro Cantore, *Verbum abbreviatum,* c. 1, *PL* 205, 25.

12. Cf. John XXIII's opening speech on October 11, 1962: *The Documents of Vatican II,* ed. W. Abbott (New York, 1966) pp. 710–719, esp. p. 716.

13. Conferenza Episcopale Italiana, *La preparazione al sacerdozio ministeriale. Orientamenti e norme* (Rome, 1972) n. 3–52 and 151. It is also worth noting the format and content of the document issued by the Sacred Congregation for Catholic Education: *The Theological Formation of Future Priests* (Rome, 1976). The National Conference of Catholic Bishops' *Report of the Bishops' Ad Hoc Committee for Priestly Life and Ministry* (Washington, 1974) relates this concern in scholarship to the pastoral ministry of the ordained. The whole question of the "starting" point in theological discussion formed part of the initial discussion of the 1971 Synod of Bishops' Meeting. Cf. D.Wuerl, *The Catholic Priesthood Today* (Chicago, 1976).

14. Cf. *Optatam totius*, n. 3.

15. R. Vander Gucht, H. Vorgrimler (ed.) *Bilan de la théologie du XXe siecle* (Paris, 1970), vol. 1.

16. Brescia, 1970.

17. This classification has a certain affinity with a terminology that historically goes back to the last phase of D. Bonhoeffer's theology; we do not wish, however, to go into the discussion of what sense Bonhoeffer himself understood the similar expressions used by him.

18. A classical example is that of E. Mersch, *La théologie du corps mystique* (Paris, 1946).

19. Y. M. Congar's work, *The Mystery of the Temple* (Westminster, 1962) is an example of the theology of the biblical conception of the divine presence of the people of God, even if the title does not express it.

20. D. Catarzi, *Teologia delle missioni estere* (Parma, 1958); W. H. Dodd, "Toward a Theology of Priesthood," in: *Theological Studies* 28 (1967), 683–705; the works mentioned in our bulletin on "Il problema teologico della predicazione," in: *Gregorianum* 40 (1959) 671–744, and in the one of D. Grasso, "Nuovi apporti alla

teologia della predicazione," in: *Gregorianum* 44 (1964) pp. 88–118; Y. M. Congar, *Jalons pour une théologie du laïcat* (Paris, 1954).

21. K. Rahner, "Theology of Poverty" in *Theological Investigations* Vol. VIII, pp. 168–214.

22. E.g., *Theological Dictionary* by K. Rahner and H. Vorgrimler, Eng. trans. (New York, 1965); *Dictionary of New Testament Theology* (3 vols.), ed. C. Brown (Exeter, 1975–78). *The Teaching of Christ*, R. Lawler, D. Wuerl, T. Lawler, (Huntington, 1976).

23. *Towards a Theology of Development, An Annotated Bibliography* compiled by Fr. Gerhard Bauer, for Sodepax (Geneva, 1970).

24. An example of this dogmatic implication in the ethical problem is to be found in chap. 3 (part I) of *Gaudium et spes*, in which, seeking the norm of human activity in the universe, there is recourse in nearly every paragraph to the concept of "the will of the Creator," "the intention of God," "God's creative plan"; e.g., *Gaudium et spes*, n. 35.

25. *Gaudium et spes*, n. 4, 11.

26. *Optatam totius*, n. 16.

27. Cf., e.g., Leonardo Lessio, *De perfectionibus moribusque divinis* (Antwerp, 1620).

28. Cf. Z. Alszeghy and M. Flick, *Metodologia per una teologia dello sviluppo* (Brescia, 1970), pp. 94–9.

29. *Gaudium et spes*, n. 43.

30. M. Flick, "La svolta antropologica in teologia," in: *La Civiltà Cattolica* 121 (1970/IV), pp. 218–20.

5

Synthesis

Primitive man saw the world as a living unit in which phenomena were only manifestations of occult forces, which permeated everything, even man himself. Each part of this universe was connected with all the others; every event had repercussions, through a mysterious sympathy, in all other beings.

Scientific culture was born[1] when man began to free individual phenomena from the meshes of this unitarian and dynamic view, identifying the center of the various functions in the substance itself as one and distinct from other beings. Thought opposes the thinking subject to the known object and takes possession of it in a certain sense through knowledge. Natural sciences began with the description of objects and of their essences that ground the laws of nature. History lists the events of the past, indicating the principal characters, their development, their causes, their effects. Psychology distinguishes acts, discovers their roots in the "faculties," and behind all that intuits the subject. Logic isolates concepts in the flux of thoughts, composes them in judgments, from which it constructs reasoning. The ideal of this process is perfect *analysis*, by which the universe is broken down into its ultimate elements.

Gradually it was understood that all this analytical work is possible since it includes, more or less explicitly, its reverse, *synthesis*.

The world, in fact, is not composed of monads, but of beings, which exist in mutual and dynamic relationship, so much so that the meaning of things depends on their functionality, that is, on the way in which they are inserted in the structure of the dynamic relations that make up the universe.[2] Historical events are manifestations of the process through which communities and persons, challenged by the internal and external situation, develop, are destroyed or, in many cases, change. Psychical life is not an accumulation of incidents gathered on an underlying spiritual substance, but a continual and complex flux of attitudes and ways of behaving that construct the personality. Concepts are the result of an abstraction that can never render all the riches of direct perception.

Reality is not a thing, or an accumulation of things, but a structure, that is, an orderly whole, in which the elements are interdependent to such an extent that when one is changed they are all modified. When scientific knowledge realizes the structural nature of reality, and turns explicitly (beyond analysis) to synthesis, the evolution of scientific thought makes a spiral. Owing precisely to the thoroughness of the analysis, the knowing mind goes beyond mere analysis and rediscovers once more the unity of the multiple. The latter, however, will no longer be the magic universe of primitive man, but a structure, that is, a plurality of beings, which could not exist and would have no meaning if they were not united with one another through reciprocal relations.

Synthesis, that is, the operation through which the unity of the multiple is noted, is neither a direct perception (the relationships are not "seen"), nor a reasoning (the relations are not the outcome of a deduction or of an induction). The structure is grasped through an *intuition*. Contrary to what is often thought, intuition is an *objective* cognition, which discovers what actually exists. In like manner, synthesis is not a subjective construction, like the figure that is composed by putting colored stones together, following one's fancy. Intuition is, moreover, a cognition that for the most part *matures* only with great effort. One becomes aware of the unity after having gathered, carefully observed, and compared the individual parts; the spontaneous and immediate discovery is only the end of a process of research. If an intuition seems to be irrational or mysterious, this happens only because the *rational* process of research, of which it is the result, is sometimes carried out partly unconsciously.

Synthesis, as the intuitive discovery of structural unity in the multiple, is of very great value in all sciences. However, a science, by its very nature, cannot stop at the synthesis grasped intuitively, without working it out in such a way that it can be communicated to and be verified by others. In fact, the essential property of scientific research is the communicability and verifiability of the results.

In a science, therefore, synthesis must become an object of reflection, through which the order of the elements is described in the way of a "form," putting in brackets the actual identity of the single elements that compose it, as when an ethnographer describes a popular dance disregarding the names and the individual qualities of the dancers. In this way the structure grasped intuitively is objectivized, and the set of functional relations among the various elements becomes a model that can be transferred and applied also to other cases. After this operation, knowledge of the original structure receives a new dimension since, considering the single elements, they are revealed as elements of the synthesis. In this way the synthesis is proved true in its applicability to the elements that constitute it. To make things clear, we call the synthesis described reflectively and applied to its elements a *system*.[3]

Synthesis — The Task of Theology

The formation of a system is therefore the goal of scientific work, and therefore also of theological study. The golden ages of the history of theology, in fact, were the ones in which unity, grasped instinctively at the prescientific level of ecclesial life, was reconstituted after having been analyzed in theological study into a whole according to the theologians' view of things. This order once again became the object of reflection and demonstration and at the same time a source of deeper knowledge of the Christian mystery. In no other period, perhaps, was this unity so clearly worked out as in the second half of the thirteenth century, thanks mainly to St. Thomas, who is rightly considered a thinker of structured multiplicity, that is, of order.[4] In the thoughts of Thomas Aquinas, in fact, not only are the single doctrines described and better understood in their synthetic unity, but also the relations of theological science with theological life, on the one hand, and with human sciences, on the other, result in a theology that is the soul of a culture of fascinating unity.

At present, on the contrary, the criticism most frequently raised against the theological science of our time is precisely the lack of a new synthesis, adapted to the present state of ecclesial consciousness, to present-day knowledge of theological sources and to the contemporary cultural situation.

It is easy to see that the mutual relationship of the *various* theological *assertions* today is little studied. Apart from manuals, postulated by didactical requirements, the *Summa* can now be considered an extinct species. The most outstanding theologians express their thought in the form of articles, which are subsequently gathered in a volume. It could be said that today the only way of presenting theological knowledge as a whole is that of an encyclopedia in alphabetical order.

The lack of synthesis between the *various theologies* is even more deeply felt. In an eminently pluralistic cultural situation, their diversity cannot but be marked. In fact, it is almost impossible to express the theories formed in a given context of ecclesial thought, in the intellectual language of another Catholic theology. In the lack of the possibility of comparison (and therefore of control), the Church herself runs the risk of seeming to be "a club for theological discussions" in which the unity of the confession of faith seems to disappear. Unity between *knowledge and real-life existence* is even more in crisis. At present, scientific theology, taught in universities and seminaries, has little to do with the life of prayer, with community commitment, with the search for the life-style of future priests, and with preparation for the various functions of pastoral activity. The recriminations of students often point out that the recommendations of the Council for a synthesis between science, spiritual life, and the priestly ministry, are still far from being put into practice.[5]

It would be very naïve to explain the present lack of synthesis as if it were the effect of inability or bad will. The development of culture proceeds in a pendulous way, swinging now to the analytical function, now to the synthetic one. In view of the enormous increase in knowledge and consequently in problems, it is quite natural that we should find ourselves in a situation in which every system inevitably appears insufficient to organize the whole of theological knowledge.

In the search for a synthesis, we must avoid the "primitivistic" illusion, which would like to return to prereflexive unity, abandoning analysis. Such romantic returns, apart from other points of view, are not possible. Persons whose intellectual lives proceed in conformity with scientific civilization and modern technique, cannot abstain from asking questions about the exact meaning and the ultimate causes of their views of the world. Nor can a synthesis be expected from information that has arrived from outside, by means of a book or a course of lectures. The knowledge acquired in this way is not sufficient to give a synthesis because it is nothing but a new analytical element added to the others, even if it can, of course, guide the mind to create its own synthesis.

The synthesis germinates, insofar as the analytical parts are constantly examined under the aspect of their unity, which they virtually contain. It is born when the unity of some essential elements in the structure of reality is grasped intuitively. It progresses, when one reflects how new elements are integrated in the synthesis, and how the synthesis itself is modified through assimilation of these new elements.

Synthesis Among Doctrines

Speaking of synthesis in theology, one thinks in the first place of the one that determines the structure of the assertions worked out in theological research. In the history of theology, we meet various models through which these syntheses were constructed. Of course, these schemata were not created all at once. They are the fruits of progressive concentration, since in the encyclopedic collections of affirmations, certain groups of assertions referring to identical or kindred objects emerged.[6] For mnemonic or literary requirements, more and more extensive articulations were accentuated. In this way were progressively formed three principal models, which can be applied to all theological material.

The first systematic model is inspired by the *history of salvation,* although it is far more ancient than the term that has come into fashion recently. Assertions are conceived as the elements of a story that follows the *temporal order* according to which the various mysteries came about in the history of humanity. It begins with God's intimate life, conceived, according to the model of John 17:5, as a story that took place "before the world was made." There follows the creation, sin, and redemption, that is, the past insofar as it illuminates the present of mankind, to which is added the present age, with the description of Christian life (morality) and the aids that make it possible (the sacraments). The picture closes with the history of the future, that is, with eschatology.

This is the synthesis, which is already seen in some Creeds[7] which animated various systematic attempts of the patristic age[8] and became the favorite systematic starting point of medieval doctrines.[9] Through Peter Lombard's *Liber Sententiarum,* the historical synthesis influenced the classical treatises of post-Tridentine theology, even if the historical orientation were generally not consciously accepted and completely applied. The situation changed after World War II, when theology reassessed the idea of the history of salvation and found in it the ideal framework for present-day theology.[10] The Council accepted this orientation, and it desired that not only dogmatic theology, but also "other theological disciplines should be renewed by livelier contact with the mystery of Christ and the history of salvation."[11]

In fact, the historical synthesis has undeniable advantages. The historical view, and only this view, can explain why the mystery of Christ is the center of created reality, and the only explanation of man's mysterious existence.[12] In fact, an essentialistic and a historical view of reality and salvation cannot see in Christ's gift anything but an incidental corrective of existence, and is not capable of seeing in it the decisive turning point of human existence. Furthermore, in the historical view, dogmatic theology (and in a certain sense moral theology) proceed in a parallel way with biblical theology, so that Scripture really becomes the soul of systematic theology. Finally, this synthesis places the mysteries in that order in which their revelation became necessary for the people of God. In this way therefore it is easier to avoid the imposition of solutions before the questions to which the latter offer a reply are understood.

However, the historical systematic principle also has *disadvantages* that are not negligible, so much as that in the last few years there has been a slight decline in its use.

In the first place, there are very important theological doctrines that cannot be fitted into this schema because they extend over the whole history of salvation and constitute its constant horizon. Such, for example, is the teaching on grace and the theological virtues. Medieval theologians sometimes dealt with this in connection with the Old Testament (since the patriarchs were justified by faith), sometimes in connection with Christology (because Christ is the source of all supernatural life), sometimes also in the context of contemporary life (as the content of Christian vocation).[13] The systematic placing of supernatural gifts is not without importance in their understanding. The error, for example, according to which the just in the Old Testament did not have grace but pleased God only through their works (the source of a latent Pelagianism, which is, however, not infrequent in persons superficially informed in theology), is a consequence of the rigidly "historical" systematic concept, sin-Christ-grace.

More serious is the fact that present-day theologians cannot avoid the problem as to what extent certain "historical" approaches to Sacred Scriptures refer to an external history that can be determined chronologically, and to what extent they represent with a dramatic scene, permanent structures, or refer to the process of interior becoming, through which personal existence is constructed. There are events presented in Sacred Scripture in the way of a story that takes place in time but that cannot be placed in the mainstream of time. Examples are the drama of Eden and the persecution and final victory of the Church described in Revelation. If these mysteries are fixed at a point of the synthesis that follows the order of temporal succession, there is the possibility of misunderstanding that confuses the parable and history, external and internal, becoming, "horizontal" history that can be measured with time and "vertical" history that refers to the existence of the person.[14]

It does not seem, therefore, that *all* theological assertions can be placed *only* in the one-dimensional line of becoming, according to the order of "before" and "after" that can be measured with time. These difficulties must not be exaggerated, however, in such a way as to cause us to forget that the concept of the history of salvation has exceptional systematic force in theology. Human, personal, and community salvation, as a task to be accomplished in an existence incarnate in matter, the tension between sin and redemption, death and resurrection — essential elements in Catholic faith — cannot be concretely conceived in categories that disregard historicity. The discovery of the history of salvation as one of the synthesizing principles of the understanding of faith, is, therefore, a definitive acquisition of theology.

Another systematic model follows *the order of the concepts dealt with.* In Western thought, concepts are mostly organized in pyramidal form, descending from the very general genus to the lowest species, through successive divisions, carried out by adding to the concepts more and more particular specific differences. We find an example in one of the authors of the literary genre of the *Summa,* Philip the Chancellor, who divides his great systematic work according to differences in the concept of "bonum." He deals first with good in general, then with good in particular, subdividing it into uncreated good and created good. In the latter, he distinguishes the good of nature and that of grace, in which he passes from the grace of angels to that of humans, and in human grace he stresses the further distinction between the grace that transforms man (gratia gratum faciens) and the grace that disposes to works (gratia gratis data).[15] The unpublished anonymous *Medieval Summa,* contained in *Cod. Vat. Lat.* 4305, embraces all theological knowledge, subdividing the notion of good by means of fourteen articles subordinated to one another, in more than six hundred chapters.

Another form of pyramidal system arranges theological data according to the degree of perfection in which they participate in an absolute exemplary model. This concept puts at the top of the pyramid not the most generic concept, but the one that expresses greatest perfection, while the base of the pyramid is constituted by the beings that are the images most distant from the supreme prototype. The schema of gradual participation on the infinite was a favorite way of Neoplatonists to conceive the universe,[16] and it appears also in theological works,[17] but it has never been able to supply the fabric of a whole major systematic work.[18]

The pyramidal systematic model offers great advantages, in fact, creating a theological synthesis. In the first place, it is capable of accepting the whole of theological material, which is very heterogeneous, and of classifying it progressively in depth, according to the same structural principle, without treating the same concept in different parts of the system. (This is precisely the reason why a variant of the model, the decimal system, is preferred in organizing library catalogues and some files.) Its disadvantage is that it presupposes the univocity of concepts and does not facilitate the correct use of biblical and patristic material.

The latter can be introduced into the system only after its interpretations in a univocal and formalized theological terminology, which inevitably impoverishes the riches of the revealed message. For this reason it is difficult to insert it this system reflections on concrete, or unrepeatable events, which, in their complex individuality, can be considered from various conceptual standpoints: for example, the way in which Christ's passion is integrated in the system already stresses a particular determined meaning of this event,[19] and therefore tends to neglect others, which are equally important.

The pyramidal form is not, however, the only way possible to organize the order of concepts. Another way is to organize thoughts by opposing two *correlative concepts*, which explain and complete each other. By choosing the correlative pairs according to all the senses of the correlativity, which are possible in a given subject matter, it is possible to circumscribe a field of knowledge perfectly, as a traveler determines the position of an island he has discovered by indicating the extreme points of north and south, east and west.[20]

The authors of the New Testament inherited from the synagogue the technique of explaining a complex reality by dichotomies or bipolar presentations. Especially in the theology of St. Paul and St. John, pairs of correlative concepts are of great importance. Let us think, for example, of the opposition between flesh and spirit, life and death, sin and justice, slavery and freedom, works and faith, darkness and light, falsehood and truth, Adam-Christ, Old Law-New Law — and examples could easily be multiplied. It is natural that subsequent theology should adopt these antitheses to develop its synthesis.

Traces of the correlative conceptual system are already found in the traditional systematic division, in which "signs" are opposed to "realities," and among the latter a distinction is made between those that are pleasant and those that are useful.[21] When St. Thomas divides his *Summa* according to the idea of *exitus* and *reditus*, adding a third part on Christ, the way for the creatures' return to God, he likewise follows the model of correlative ideas.[22]

At present, the synthetic structure based on correlative concepts appears more frequently in works of Protestant authors than in those of Catholic theologians. While Catholic theology, polemical with regard to its scholastic past, in fact, tries to emancipate itself from philosophical categories and so turns more toward historical and biblical conceptions, the theology of the Reformation, reacting in a similar way against its own past, is more aware of the advantages that philosophy offers to assimilate intellectually the content of revelation.

The classic author of the correlative method is Paul Tillich, and it is natural, therefore, that correlativity should influence his work more deeply. Tillich distinguishes three points of view of correlativity in the theological field: (1) the correspondence between symbols and their significance, (2) the polarity of the concepts referring to God and to man, and (3) the interdependency of structural requirements and their object.[23] The division of Tillich's *Systematic Theology* into five parts (each of which is subdivided into two parallel parts) is a deeply thought-out combination of these categories.

The schema of correlative concepts is so congenial to contemporary thought that it appears even in works that do not explicitly set out to use it. A significant example is found in Vatican Council II, which recommends the synthetic value of the history of salvation for the unification of theology. When, however, it formulates the document nearest to the modern outlook, that is, *Gaudium et spes*, the *Pastoral Constitution on the Church in the Modern World*, it hardly mentions the history of salvation but repeatedly follows the dialectics of correlative concepts. The questions of the world are opposed, in fact, to the answers of faith, the general structures of human reality to the solutions of particular problems, the essential image, and the historico-existential reality of human activity in the world.

With concepts arranged in this way, the difficulties of including in one system permanent structures and historical events are certainly diminished. However, the validity of the correlation, as a principle of synthesis, depends on whether it is possible to find in it a reason for beginning the exposition starting from a given concept and then passing on in a given order to other correlative relationships. In our opinion, this reason cannot be discovered on the basis of the principle itself. Just as anyone who wishes to draw various diameters in a circle can begin at any point of the circumference, and can continue in any direction, so the correlative conception does not purpose any obligatory starting point or mandatory direction. Therefore, the principle of correlation can certainly render great service in investigating some particular topic, but alone it does not provide a structure to organize all theological material.

The examination of the various systematic models has brought us to a negative verdict: none of them seems suitable to inspire the order for a future *Summa Theologica.* This judgment is confirmed apparently by examination of the few existing systematic works that seem to proceed eclectically, combining various organizing systems. When we examine the structure of these works, however, there emerges a third systematic model, which is actually present in them all.

Let us take as an example the "theological aesthetics" of H. U. von Balthasar.[24] This work begins with a volume on supernatural knowledge; a second one gathers monographic expositions on how the theme of "glory" was treated by a series of thinkers; a third moves "in the space of metaphysics"; and a fourth is dedicated to the teaching of the Old Testament. It is expected that successive volumes will deal again with the New Testament, and finally a specific theory of the author will be set forth. In this schema, which is not at all linear, there is actually present one constant concern, which guides the order of the treatment: to construct slowly a way toward the correct formulation and solution of the problem that interests the author. In fact, the reflections on knowledge, the monographic expositions, the comparison between theology and metaphysics, and the reading of the Old Testament, must be treated in this order and in no other, not because of the mutual relationship between the objects themselves, but because the subjective thought winds along this way precisely in order to raise and to solve a specific question. The systematic principle of the whole work is, therefore, the *dynamism of knowledge,* which grasps a problem intuitively, works out the instruments of research (mental categories, models of thought, and hypotheses), and concentrically limits the field of obscure indeterminateness, moving toward understanding.

Apropos of the path of knowledge, the allusion is not, therefore, to the deductive and inductive movement of a line of reasoning, but to the psychological and gnosiological maturing of faith, which progressively finds more and more understanding of itself. In this penetration, *use is also made* of the analysis of conceptual systems (pyramidal and correlative) and *also* of reflection on historical facts that followed one another in time, in such a way, however, that the guiding thread is greater and greater intellectual penetration.

The model of the synthesis inspired by the dynamism of knowledge is not an unprecedented novelty. In a certain way, it already appears in St. Bonaventure's *Journey of the Soul to God,* the systematic order of which was discussed for decades precisely because it cannot be set in any previous schema.[25] The synthesis created under the aspect of the march of knowledge is verified in a certain sense, because it gives the key to understand works of unquestionable value, which otherwise would seem nothing but an eclectic, in fact capricious, collection of chapters. We are thinking, for example, of the schema of a dogmatic theology, conceived by Karl Rahner,[26] or of the anthropology of Rheinhold Niebuhr, one of the best-known systematic theologians in the English-speaking world.[27]

The synthesis envisaged from the standpoint of the progressive dynamism of knowledge explains the proposal to reorganize all dogmatic teaching according to the stages of the evolution of the dogmas.[28] In the first year of theology, students would acquire an understanding of the life of the apostolic community with its Old Testament roots, considering also the first confessions of faith, which were already beginning to appear. In the second year, they would study the theology of the Church Fathers, concentrating on their trinitarian and Christological doctrine. In the third year they would come into touch with medieval dogmatics and that of the Council of Trent, stress being laid on their sacramental and anthropological orientation. In the fourth year they would have the opportunity to read contemporary theologians and to do personal research.

Personally, from the didactic standpoint, we do not think that this schema is a suitable one, because historical development does not coincide with the progress of personal reflection: this identification is one of the weak points of the Hegelian system. In fact, the development of the theology of the past was determined by historical factors completely alien to the intellectual life of the modern student (Neoplatonism, Manicheism, Jansenist rigor,). But the very fact of a proposal of such a didactic system shows what an attraction the dynamico-gnosiological model exercises in our time. That is quite natural because theology, in our opinion, is not in the first place a static *structure* of assertions but a dynamic structure of research. Therefore, the principle that the *synthesis* underlines (and which acts as the pivot of the *system*), must come not from the relationship of objective realities

but from the order of the activity of the subject, who seeks understanding of faith.

Synthesis in Theological Pluralism

A second form of synthesis, necessary for the critical interpretation of ecclesial life, tries to understand the relationship between the
various theological systems and the opposite theological assertions
appearing in the different theological movements existing in the
unity of the Church.[29]

Let us begin with the fact that many believers have the impression that a *new phenomenon* has been taking place in ecclesial life in
the last decade. The unbroken uniformity with which all Catholics
firmly adhered to the same formulas of faith, which was one of the
apologetic arguments for the truth of the Catholic Church as compared with the division of Protestantism, and which attracted a good
many people to Catholicism between World War I and World War II,
seems lost today. Concepts and terms, which had for centuries been
considered suitable instruments to express the Christian mystery,
(hypostatic union, transubstantiation, nature, person, matter and form
the sacraments) are rejected as things of the past. Dogmas defined in
ecumenical councils are being questioned and are denied by persons
who profess to be Catholics (divinity of Christ, original sin, the effi-
ciency "ex opere operato" of the sacraments, the necessity of confession, eternal life). Nor can it be said that the diversity is limited to
theories. The validity of forms of behavior, traditionally considered
postulates of the law of Christ, is questioned.

Theologians propose various explanations of the mystery of salvation. These explanations start from different points of view, use different methods, and adopt different languages — to such an extent
that not only does the believer without a theological formation fail to
understand them, but also the representatives of the various
movements themselves ignore one another and are incapable of
dialoguing with one another.

In the first half of the century, it was very easy, by referring to
the Magisterium, to distinguish between "necessary" assertions
(which everyone had to accept) and "free" questions (in which discussion was possible), fixing carefully the "theological note" of every
assertion. But today the role the Magisterium actually plays in ecclesial life has changed. On the one hand, theology hardly expects that
the Magisterium should indicate unifying frameworks. Theology is

considered in fact (more or less explicitly) a critical science, which does not confine itself just to explaining and defending the teaching of the hierarchy, but takes the initiative for the comparison of the sources with the forms of thought and with present-day problems, suggesting to the Magisterium how and what it should preach. On the other hand, the ecclesiastical authority does not intervene to repress existing pluralism, and only with great circumspection and very rarely does it take up a position against theories, which, in the opinion of the faithful, is considered as being in flagrant contrast with their own faith.

The variety of opinions is so broad and intense that the believer may have the impression that the teaching of certain non-Catholic thinkers expresses more faithfully an adherence to the Father through Christ in the Spirit than the theories of some authors who are, nevertheless, recognized as Catholic theologians.

The problem is whether it is possible to discover in this multiplication of disagreements a structure that can be drawn with a synthesis and developed in a system.

To answer this question, let us begin by comparing the present situation with the *pluralism of the past*. On reading the various books of the Old and the New Testaments, we see not only the difference of style, but also the different ways of presenting the truths that God has willed to communicate to us for our salvation. Referring to the Gospels, Vatican Council II reminds us that the sacred authors, "in writing the four Gospels, selected certain of the many elements which had been handed on, either orally or already in written form, others they synthesized or explained with an eye to the situation of the churches, the while sustaining the form of preaching, but always in such a fashion that they have told us the honest truth about Jesus."[30]

It is understandable, therefore, how there exists a pluralism (not contradictory but complementary) in the image of Jesus presented to us by the four evangelists, and how exegetes are more and more opposed to efforts to try to condense, with typographical devices, the four Gospels into one, doing violence to the specific perspective of the individual evangelists. It has long been pointed out, too, that, in the expounding of the essential teachings of Christianity, there is a different accentuation in the same inspired authors, due to their different temperaments and to different circumstances.

Rousselot already pointed out that, while for St. John the grace given to us by Christ appears above all as raising us above our condition as creatures. In St. Paul, on the contrary, Christ's gift is seen particularly as a liberation from the sin that dwells in us.[31] The polemics against the insistence that Christians first become Jews drove St. Paul to lay such stress on the gratuitousness of divine mercy and the futility of observance of the law as to give rise to false interpretations, deplored by the Apostle himself (Rom. 3:8), and corrected in James's letter, in which emphasis is laid on the necessity that good works should accompany a sincere faith (James 2:14–26). We must recognize, therefore, that not even the preaching of the Apostles was completely monolithic. If we must speak today of a theology of St. John, of St. Paul, of St. Luke, it is precisely because of the pluralism of the inspired writers, which gives us a richer knowledge of Christ and his message, seen from more than one angle.

When specifically theological reflection on faith begins, as happened with the patristic age, pluralism deepens. There continues to exist pluralism due to a different accentuation of the various aspects of the Christian message. Just think of the way in which the theology of grace is formed in the East and in the West. While the Greek Fathers develop extensively all the aspects of the "divinization" of the baptized Christian who is united to the Holy Spirit,[32] in the West, on the contrary, justification is conceived dynamically, from St. Augustine, as the effect of an action of God in man, which gradually frees him from the slavery of lust, a liberation that will be complete only in the eschatological state.[33]

We find, however, also another kind of pluralism, derived from the different philosophical conceptions used to explain the truths of faith. A typical example of this pluralism appears in the explanations successively given of union with Christ, which is necessary to participate in redemption.

Faith teaches that all people without exception are united with Christ, and that they are saved inasmuch as they accept in some way this union with faith and baptism, and live under the influence of Christ, which, as the Council of Trent teaches, "always precedes, accompanies, and follows the good works of the just, and without which these works cannot in any way be pleasing to God and meritorious (DS 1546). The Greek Fathers explained the radical union of all people with Christ on the basis of Platonic doctrines, according to which there exists an identical human nature in single individuals, different only accidentally. Later, up to recent times, stress was laid on the fact that individuals belonged to a single family, descending from one father, Adam.

As for Christ's continual influence in the just man, the Fathers express it particularly by emphasizing the similarity with Christ, impressed by the Holy Spirit, and the union that is established between the Christian and the body of Christ, in the eucharistic communion, the effects of which they describe very realistically. Scholastics have recourse to Aristotelian causes, recognizing in Christ the final, efficient, and exemplary cause of our sanctification and attributing a certain instrumental causality to Christ's humanity in the production of the grace created.

In this example we see how the same truth of faith is preserved and expressed in very different ways, sometimes incompatible with one another, depending on convictions extraneous to faith. It could be said that, when these convictions are proved to be wrong, the explanations themselves would collapse. (For example, when it is proved that Platonic realism is untenable, it could no longer be said that Christ is united indirectly with all people by assuming a human nature.) However, the proof of the falsity of the different theories would not enter specifically the theological field, in which the various explanations of union with Christ would keep at least a hypothetical value for those who could not be convinced by philosophical or scientific proofs.

In the period of Neo-Scholastic theology, the pluralism of theological schools was restricted to especially difficult particular questions. It is true that, in the great masters, it has very deep roots of a philosophical nature (the way of conceiving being or transcendency and the freedom of God, or the value of human acts in the construction of moral personality). From the end of the nineteenth century, however, they all speak a common language so that it is very easy to localize the "adversaries" of a given thesis, as can be seen from Neo-Scholastic manuals. Molinists and Thomists battle over the possibility of "scientia media" (the knowledge that God has of futurables, of what one would do if one were placed in circumstances difference from those in which one lives), well knowing on both sides what they respectively affirm or deny. The same happens when Scotists affirm that, to be really just, it is not enough to have habitual grace; it is also necessary to be accepted by God as just. The Thomists reply that there is no need of this divine acceptance because the presence of grace in man is already the effect of the love with which God loves him as just.

During the last hundred years, in the period between the two Vatican Councils, theological pluralism was reduced to the minimum. The Pauline postulate of the "same mind and the same judgment" (1

Cor. 1:10), interpreted in a requirement of uniformity, became a disciplinary rule. The causes of the unification of theological thought were the psychology of the besieged fortress, threatened by the assaults of modern thought;[34] the strong centralization, with which the Holy See bade everyone follow the most certain opinions, in teaching and in research;[35] and a poor historical sense, as a result of which it was considered rash to abandon opinions commonly accepted in the past. All these factors appeared united and intensified in the reaction against modernism,[36] and they continued in some way until the condemnation of the "new theologies."[37]

It certainly cannot be said that this monolithic period was particularly propitious to the development of theology. The authors of that period who are most quoted today are rather the ones who were outside a unity that seems artificial to us today.

Turning to the cultural situation today, we understand that long-standing theological pluralism cannot help being incomparably more marked.

In a certain sense, the spread of pluralism in theology can be explained, paradoxically, with the development of hermeneutics in the last few decades. The pursuit of the understanding of faith necessarily implies continual recourse to the sources. To do so effectively, theologians should use extremely complex philosophical, historiographical, and philosophical equipment. They should adopt the point of view of various sciences. Evidently, this work cannot be done by one person alone. The specialist in systematic theology must inevitably accept the results of the research of others. But individual specialists in the auxiliary sciences rarely agree. Affirmations described as "the result of modern science," if they do not refer to generalities, mostly absolutize the opinion of some particular movement. Therefore, because the science of interpretation is going through a phase of intense and very rapid growth, the probability of disagreement on the meaning of the individual sources of theology has greatly increased.

A further explanation of today's pluralism lies in that characteristic of modern theology we described when speaking of theologies "with genitive of subject." The understanding of faith uses categories and convictions widespread in the cultural world in which it is developed; otherwise theologians would have to leave the world to exercise their trade, and the result of their research could not be assimilated in the intellectual context in which they live. Once, when the cultural environment was relatively homogeneous, this adaptation differentiated theology from the previous phases of this research, but ensured a new synchronous unity. The theological thought of Scholastics in the second half of the thirteenth century or of the seventeenth century was relatively less pluralistic because it was adapted to a predominating homogeneous culture.

Today, on the contrary, culture is no longer one. In spite of easy contacts by means of the various media of communication, the intellectual world of various peoples, of various classes, of generations, of groups, is dominated by different philosophies and ideologies. Therefore the various theologies, constituted in dialogue with these intellectual movements that do not understand one another, are more different than ever from one another. Because theology wishes to be able to dialogue with a pluralistic world, it must renounce being a homogeneous science, equally accessible to everyone, in the formulation of its problems, in terminology, in the solutions it proposes.

A source of inevitable pluralism is also that trend of present-day theology that tries to discover the religious sense of the profane reality in which the believer is immersed. The theology "with genitive of the object" necessarily implies a determined view of the reality studied. As Vatican Council II points out, it may happen that, while some faithful think their Christian vision of reality suggests a certain solution, "it happens rather frequently, and legitimately so, that some of the faithful, with no less sincerity, will see the problem quite differently." The Council concludes from this that "they ought to remember that in those cases no one is permitted to identify the authority of the Church exclusively with his own opinion."[38] In fact, if among believers there may be followers of various sociological, political trends, etc. (as is evident), it follows that the theological judgment on the situation, which presupposes one or another interpretation of reality, can be different.

Finally, pluralism is a postulate of the possibility of conceiving *various syntheses* among the various theological doctrines. In fact, theological understanding in the schema of the history of salvation, or conceived according to the model of a conceptual system, or even centered on the dynamic progress of knowledge, is different. Even if these theologies agree on all controversial questions, they will differ at least in that they conceive in a different way the relationship of the various propositions contained in the common faith. For the meaning of a phrase, the linguistic and logical context in which it is inserted is not an indifferent matter. Therefore, attempts repeated on several occasions in the past to reorganize the theses of a theologian in the systematic order of another, are rightly considered unfruitful, since they do violence to the unity of thought expounded by various authors.[39]

On the basis of the testimony of history and considering the present cultural situation, we can construct a synthesis according to which the plurality of theologies is revealed not as chaos, but as a structure.

In the first place theological pluralism is an inevitable consequence of the disproportion between the limited nature of the human intellect and "the mystery of Christ, which, though it is a mystery of recapitulation and universal reconciliation, goes beyond the possibility of expression of any period of history, and thus lies outside all exhaustive systematization."[40] In particular, theological uniformity is incompatible with the adaptations of the Christian message to various cultures, which is necessary for the universal mission of the Church.[41] Without an accepted and desired theological pluralism, the Church would end by shutting herself up in a ghetto. Therefore, the precepts that the Council gives with regard to the respect due to the specific character of separated Eastern theologians in setting forth the mysteries,[42] must be applied to theological pluralism within the Catholic Church. It is inevitable, in fact, that there should be theological trends that are not only different and complementary, but also opposite. They cannot all be true. In fact the risk of error is an inevitable condition of serious research.

It must be added, however, that an acceptable plurality must not be a definitive, stationary difference, but a plurality in *movement, toward unity*. The unifying dynamism is realized at two levels, in two different ways.

In the first place, the contradictory plurality of assertions, *which exclude one another* absolutely, which inevitably implies that least one of the assertions is wrong, must be accepted only as an evil to be overcome. The progress of theology faces the risk of error, but tries to eliminate error, and constructs formulas that unite the grains of truth contained in contradictory sentences.

In the second place, the plurality of *different but not contradictory* assertions must be kept, but the analysis of each assertion must be carried to the point at which it is realized that one does not exclude, but on the contrary completes, the other. The unification of this second sense does not aim therefore at the suppression of differences but at understanding of unity in diversity.

Of course, at the first meeting with an opinion different from ours, it is generally not possible to know if it is a question of a contradictory difference or merely a complementary one. Therefore, also in connection with the tendency of pluralism toward unity, it is necessary to apply what the Council recommends for the ecumenical movement.[43] In particular, pluralism on its way toward unity finds its vital environment in the *dialogue* among theologians. In the dialogue there should be a sincere desire for mutual understanding, even if one should not be afraid to declare openly that, in one's opinion, the thesis expounded by someone goes against the perennial faith of the Church, saving the good faith of each.

This does not mean invoking a condemnation of this or that author, but it expresses one's own judgment in order to bring forth a thorough and clarifying answer, thus causing a theological problem to progress toward its correct solution. It may be very useful in this connection to recall the observation that St. Ignatius states as a premise to his *Spiritual Exercises* in an age in which accusations of heresy were very frequent and particularly dangerous: "It should be presupposed that every good Christian should be more ready to save the affirmations of others than to condemn them; not being able to save them, let him try to know how he understands them, and if he is mistaken in this conception, let him correct him lovingly; and if not even this should be enough, let him try every means in order that, understanding them correctly, he may be saved."[44]

The Role of the Magisterium in Synthesis

Like every synthesis, the mutual relationship between the various theologies is grasped intuitively, by virtue of an intellectual effort, and progressively, in the multiplicity of the single elements.

The process with which, through pluralism, it is necessary to aim at the structured unification of theological science, shows the necessity of the *ecclesial dimension,* characteristic of theology. Theology, in fact, is essentially an ecclesial science not only because it has its starting point in ecclesial life, and has as its aim the conscious and critical development of this life, but also because theologians must look in the ecclesial community for the term of comparison and if necessary the corrective of their particular opinions. It is in the search for a synthesis among the various theologies that it becomes clearer that the real subject of theological science is not an isolated specialist, but the community itself, and that the individual work of the theologian receives its definitive meaning insofar as it is integrated in the growing maturity of ecclesial consciousness.

To explain how this integration takes place concretely, we can apply the generic model, worked out by Vatican Council II with regard to the progress of the understanding of faith. "The tradition that comes from the Apostles makes progress in the Church, with the help of the Holy Spirit. There is a growth in insight into the realities and words that are being passed on. This comes about in various ways. It comes through the contemplation and study of believers who ponder these things in their hearts. It comes from the intimate sense of spiritual realities which they experience. And it comes from the preaching of those who have received, along with the right of succession in the episcopate, the sure charism of truth."[45]

The text indicates three aspects of progress that take place under the influence of the principal personality of all ecclesial life, the Holy Spirit: reflection, experience, and preaching of the Magisterium. In our context it is of particular importance to study *the role of the Magisterium.*

It is very important that we consider the "pastors" of the Church as neither on the same level as all the other members of the ecclesial community (whose mere notaries they would be, recording their convergences in the understanding of faith), nor as separated from the whole of the ecclesial community (operating without the others or even against the others, as a repressive force of order). On the one hand, in fact, the charism of truth they have been promised enables their intervention to protect the ecclesial community (individual theologians and the whole Christian people) from all confusion in faith. Therefore the pastors of the Church carry out, in ecclesial life, a characteristic function of service, which cannot be reduced to the function of the other members of the community.

On the other hand, since the bishops do not receive new revelations, and since it cannot be claimed that the Holy Spirit ordinarily acts independently of human means, miraculously, the Magisterium does not make the other factors of doctrinal progress superfluous, and normally cannot and must not prescind from Christian thought and experience.[46] It would be contrary to the organically communitarian nature of the Church to suppose that the bishops must necessarily and in all cases replace the function of the whole Christian people, even of specialists. Normally they use the collaboration of others, as was explicitly laid down in the discussions during Vatican Council I.[47]

These general principles determine what is the *help* that the Church can expect from the hierarchy in arriving at a synthesis of the different and partly opposed theologies.

The very ground, in which the hierarchy exercises its function as herald of the message of salvation, is the *language of faith*, which we described when dealing with the life of the Church as a linguistic event. The International Theological Commission, in its declaration in 1973 on theological pluralism, expressed itself in this connection in a very fitting way: "Dogmatic definitions usually adopt current vocabulary, and even when these definitions use apparently philosophical terms, they do not commit the Church to a particular philosophy, but only express realities which underlie common human experience and which the terms in question have made it possible to detect."[48]

Since every affirmation, which has a meaning, is also the negation of contradictory affirmations, a primary function of the hierarchy is also to say what *does not correspond* to its message, remaining, however, always in the language of faith, as just described. It is absurd, in fact, that there should exist a community of faith that cannot determine what are the necessary conditions for a person to be a member of it, indicating the limits of orthopraxy and orthodoxy implied in its own doxology. Let us quote again the observations of the Theological Commission: "Even if the present situation of the Church increases pluralism, plurality finds its limit in the fact that faith creates the communion of men in truth, which has become accessible by means of Christ. This makes inadmissible any conception of faith, reducing it to a purely pragmatic cooperation, without community in truth. This truth is not bound to a theological system, but is expressed in the normative formulations of faith. When faced with presentations of the doctrine that are seriously ambiguous, even incompatible with the faith of the Church, the latter has the possibility of detecting the error, and the obligation of removing it, up to formal rejection of the heresy, as an extreme remedy, to safeguard the faith of the people of God."[49]

It should be noted that the Commission considers the sentence of anathema as an extreme case. Before a definitive and therefore infallible condemnation of heresy, there exist various degrees of intervention of the Magisterium which can be revised and are therefore, in a certain sense, provisional. There are sometimes opinions that, though not being clearly contrary to faith, are, however, dangerous because they can lead to consequences that are certainly false, or because they have not been sufficiently ripened, or because, owing to the cultural atmosphere prevailing in a given region, they run the risk of being understood as the negation of a truth of faith. In these cases it will be mainly the local bishop, who is better acquainted with the situation, who ought to intervene, observing the necessary prudence, and even, if necessary, imposing silence. St. Paul, after having recognized that there is nothing wrong in eating meat sacrificed to idols, went on: "If a certain food were to move my brother to sin, I would never eat meat, in order not to scandalize my brother" (cf. Rom. 8:12). One should not be surprised, therefore, if we are asked to make the sacrifice of renouncing the spread of an opinion considered dangerous for the faith of others.

It is necessary to distinguish from these cases, in which the Church moves at the level of the language of faith, the clash of the Magisterium with a theological theory, which lies *outside this linguistic context*. It would not be reasonable, in fact, to demand from the hierarchy that it should judge the compatibility of its own message with a theology set forth in the context and in the categories borrowed from some philosophical science or particular ideology. Just as the Holy Spirit does not miraculously give bishops the gift of the interpretation of languages to be able to judge the orthodoxy of a work written in a language unknown to them, so he does not necessarily enlighten them, by virtue of their office and charism, to understand and compare effectively with faith a work written in a specialized language, which they have not studied.

That does not mean, however, that the Magisterium should remain passive before such theories. It judges them, insofar as they exercise an influence outside their specialized language, and are read at the common linguistic level of the ecclesial community. Such a situation occurred, for example, at the end of the nineteenth and at the beginning of the twentieth century, when the ecclesiastical authorities curbed the premature acceptance of evolutionism (then presented as a war machine against religion), though without condemning the scientific theory itself. Since the influence of theories on communities is extremely subject to the provisional nature of a sociocultural historical situation, the stand of the Magisterium in this field will even more rarely be a definitive and immutable approval or condemnation.

Of course, the authoritative intervention of the Magisterium involves risks. Without going back to the case of Galileo, many people think today that there was too much haste in the condemnations against Rosmini. Moreover his book the *Five Wounds of the Church* has recently been reprinted and diffused with the consent of ecclesiastical authority. It seems that the attempt to suffocate the philosophical and theological thought of Rosmini had a negative influence on the development of original theological and philosophical research it Italy. The current reassessment of the reaction to the modernist crisis shows that not infrequently proceedings were taken too much in the spirit of "martial law" against authors who were honestly trying to serve the faith, without closing their eyes to new problems.[50]

The present pluralism itself constitutes a particular difficulty when it comes to judging exactly if a given theological opinion is dangerous in a given situation, or even incompatible with faith. It will therefore be necessary not only to give the author the possibility to explain himself, but also to question experts in the field who do not belong to just one school of thought. We do not think, however, that the difficulties of judging can eliminate or reduce to the minimum the role of the Magisterium, even if it will have to be exercised in different ways.

The observations made on the function of the Magisterium in theological pluralism also show in what sense the stands of the Magisterium in the past are criteria to judge whether a theory enters or not into the structure of the converging and complementary theologies that interpret the mystery.

Dogmatic definitions are definitive and final criteria, read, however, in the historical context in which they were formulated. when the hierarchy solves a concrete problem, investing all its authority in the solution of recent questions, definitions must not be considered as if they were absolutely valid axioms, without a context, but we must ask how it is possible to receive a light from the definitive solution of a problem that emerged in the past, in order to solve a problem that arises today.

Let us quote again the declaration of the International Theological Commission: "Dogmatic formulas must be considered answers to precise problems, and in this perspective they always remain true. Their constant interest is bound up with the lating relevance of the problems in question. Moreover, it must not be forgotten that the successive questions which Christians raise on the meaning of God's word with their solutions already acquired, are so vitally connected with one another that today's answers always presuppose to some extent those of yesterday, though they cannot be reduced to the latter."[51]

It is more difficult to determine in what sense that authentic but not infallible positions of the hierarchy (that is, all that the ecclesiastical authority has taught, without proposing it to the faith of the Church as belonging to revelation, with a solemn document, or with the common and constant teaching of the whole episcopal college),[52] have been, or remain, valid criteria for the synthesis of various theologies.

The specific purpose of these documents is to indicate along what ways it is opportune (or not opportune) to proceed in a particular cultural context, in order with certainty to keep the faith intact. What these documents authoritatively indicate is not so much speculative truth in itself, but rather the intellectual behavior that the believer must assume in order to remain faithful to the word of God in a given historical situation. It can therefore be said that these noninfallible documents regulate orthopraxis more directly than orthodoxy: the quality of the assent they require is rather of the practical than of the speculative order, that is, they refer to the value of the intellectual behavior it is opportune to adopt in a give context, and does not concern immediately the objective reality in itself.[53]

To say that these documents are not infallible is equivalent to saying that they may be subject to error, not only from the standpoint of speculative truth, but also as regards the opportuneness of rejecting or encouraging certain opinions. Such errors have taken place in the course of the history of the Church, but there are innumerable cases in which theology remained immune from hasty conclusions, just because of the interventions of the Magisterium.[54] It also happens that, when the cultural situation changes, a noninfallible document of the Magisterium, valid in the past, loses its validity. In fact, a better understanding of the dogma, or of the opinions compared with it, may enable the affirmation, which previously was dangerous for faith, to be embraced later without difficulty. This is the case of polygenism, wtih regard to which it was rightly said twenty-five years ago that it did not seem possible to reconcile it with the dogma of original sin (DS 3897), whereas today the compatibility of the dogma with this opinion seems to be sufficiently assumed.[55]

Unfortunately, these affirmations, admitted by all theologians, are often forgotten in practice, insofar as one either identifies all the acts of the Magisterium with an irreformable definition and thus judges scandalous the idea that these acts may be modified in certain cases, or one tends to ignore nonirreformable statements, as if one did not owe them that religious assent of will and intelligence, recommended again by Vatican Council II.[56] We find a similar case in secular life. As the episcopate of Germany in a collective pastoral letter in 1967 recalled, we are obliged to take into consideration the verdict of doctors or technicians, although we know that their opinions are not infallible. To neglect their judgment would imply serious negligence in dealing with life and goods, our own and those of others.[57]

It is just this specifically practical character of the authentic statements of the Magisterium that makes them particularly suitable to promote unity in a plurality of theologies, in the present crisis. They do not close definitively the way for research, but they help to prevent the Church from embracing theories, which in their present form, are not structured convergently. Therefore, since these theories are for the moment refractory to a synthesis, they would be harmful to unity of life in the ecclesial community.

Of course, the synthesis cannot be a product of individual efforts, coordinated by the work of the Magisterium only. The ecclesiology of today is more attentive than in the past to the importance of groups that exist in the Church and that as lesser but gradually increasing communities constitute an organic whole. The dialogue, which brings forth synthesis, must take place at all levels of the community, and that is not possible unless its institutional organs share in the dialogue.

Specialized theological reviews, which exist in all languages, national theological associations, congresses, universities, and seminaries, which contribute to the unity of theological consciousness in the various local churches, serve this purpose. Since the universal Church is not only a juridical confederation of local churches, but is in her turn a real community, with a "culture" of her own, that is, a unity of thought (particularly theological), the universal Church needs her own organs of synthesis.

In view of the spread of the press today and generalized knowledge of the main languages, international reviews of theology have already become factors of synthesis at the world level. The International Theological Commission, set up by the Holy See on the recommendation of the Synod of Bishops, is specifically a "forum" of theological dialogue on the universal scale, even if its activity is necessarily somewhat fragmentary. The international centers, dedicated to theological study, find the justification of their existence in this necessity of a universal synthesis. As in the Middle Ages Catholic universities today are also a privileged place of dialogue, since interdisciplinary research, the permanent collaboration of numerous specialists in the various branches of sacred sciences and also in profane ones, promote the incarnation of the message of salvation in a theological science in the modern sense of the word, which can become in a certain sense the soul of a universal culture.[58]

Chapter Notes

1. The distinction between primitive and analytical mentality (inspired, for example, by Levy-Bruhl) can be applied to distinguish various phases in cultural history only insofar as one or the other mentality may prevail in variable proportions.

2. In this exposition we have adopted some intuitions of H. Rombach, without following his terminology. Cf. H. Rombach, *Substanz, System, Struktur, Die Ontologie des Funktionalismus und der philosophische Hintergrund der modernen Wissenschaft* (Freiburg, 1965–66); *Strukturontologie* (Freiburg, 1971).

3. The word *system* is often used in a disparaging sense, which stresses the nonempirical character of intellectual constructions. We use the term in a neutral sense, as an orderly set of various elements, in which all the parts have a relationship of mutual dependency recognized and verified as such.

4. Cf. H. Meyer, *Thomas von Aquin, sein System und seine geistesgeschichtliche Stellung* (ed. 2, Paderborn, 1961), pp., 654–94. Also J. A. Weisheipl, O.P., *Friar Thomas d'Aquino His Life, Thought and Works* (Oxford, 1974).

5. Cf. *Optatam totius,* n. 16.

6. The phase of initial coagulation can be observed in the Spanish sentences of the seventh century, e.g., in Isidore of Seville (*PL* 83, 537–38), or Taius of Zaragoza (*PL* 80, 751–989).

7. E.g., in the so-called apostolic Creed, DS 27.

8. E.G. Gennadeus, *De ecclesiasticis dogmatibus* (*PL* 57, 979–1000); John of Damascus, *De fide orthodoxa* (*PL* 94, 781–1228).

9. The classic example is Hugh of St. Victor, *De sacramentis christianae fidei* (*PL* 176, 173–618).

10. Cf. M. Flick's programmatic articles, "La struttura del trattato De Deo creante et elevante," in: *Gregorianum* 36 (1955) pp. 284–90; "Teologia e storia della salvezza," in: *La Civiltà Cattolica* 116 (1964/III), pp. 7–17.

11. *Optatam totius,* n. 16.

12. Cf. *Gaudium et spes,* n. 22; *ibid.,* 45.

13. An intermediate and therefore ambiguous concept is found in: Peter Lombard, 3 *Sent.,* dist. 23–32.

14. Cf. also the critical remarks of W. Kasper on the work *Mysterium salutis,* in: *Theologische Revue* 65 (1969), pp. 1–6.

15. *Cod. Vat. Lat.* 7669 f. 1 rb. For other examples, cf. *Gregorianum* 27 (1946) 55.

16. Let us note, however, that the systematic principle of participation, in Neoplatonic thought is united, on the one hand, with the dynamic idea of cosmogony and, on the other hand, with the progressive enlightenment of the intellect; in this way the conception of participation involves all three systematic models reviewed here. Cf. Proclus, *Théologie platonicienne* I. 1, c. 4, ed. Saffrey-Westerink (Paris, 1968), 19; J. Trouillard, *Introduction,* in: *Proclos, Eléments de Théologie* (Paris, 1965), pp. 46–57;

R. Roques, *L'univers dionysien, Structure hiérarchique du monde selon le Pseudo-Denys* (Paris, 1954), e.g., 88.

17. Also in *S. Th.* I-II, Prol. itself, where the passing from the doctrine on God to that on free and operating man is justified with the observation that man is God's image.

18. As a curiosity let us recall the work of E. Dubois, *De exemplarismo Divino* (Rome, 1897), who constructed a plan to organize systematically all sciences, arts, and virtues on the basis of exemplarism.

19. Some are already indicated by St. Thomas, *S. Th.*, III, q. 48, a. 1–6.

20. In the system of H. Leisegang, *Denkformen* (ed. 2, Berlin, 1951), the system of correlativity corresponds to the "circular" type of thought, while the system of the history of salvation corresponds to the "linear" one, and the Prophyrean division of concepts to the pyramidal one.

21. Cf., e.g., Augustine, *De doctrina christiana*, 1.1, c.1 (*PL* 34; 19); Peter Lombard, 1 *Sent.* dist. 1, c. 1–3.

22. For the complex problems of the systematic plan of the *Summa Theologica*, c., e.g., G. Ghini, "Il contenuto e il piano della Somma Teologica," in: *S.Tommaso d'Aquino, La Somma Teologica, Traduzione e commento dei Domenicani Italiani*, 1 (Florence, 1965), pp. 163–252.

23. Cf. P. Tillich, *Systematic Theology 1* (Chicago, 1951), *Introduction*, IV, pp. 12–13.

24. H.U. Von Balthasar, *Herrlichkeit, Eine theologische Ästhetik* (Einsiedeln 1: 1961, 2: 1962, 3/1: 1965, 3/2: 1967).

25. St. Bonaventure, *Itinerarium mentis in Deum*, Op. (Quaracchi) 5, pp. 293–316.

26. K. Rahner, "Schema for a Treatise of Dogmatic Theology," in: *Theological Investigations*, vol. I (second edition, 1965), pp. 20–38.

27. R. Niebuhr, *The Nature and Destiny of Man, A Christian Interpretation* (New York, 1953).

28. Similar didactic systems have been proposed various times, in various forms, recently, for example, cf. K. H. Neufeld, "Theologische Ausbildung heute, ein neues Modell," in: *Theologisch praktische Quartalschrift* 120 (1972), pp. 43–51.

29. Cf.: the Document of the International Theological Commission on *Unity of Faith and Theological Pluralism*, in: *Documentation Catholique*, no. 1632 (May 20, 1973), or *La Civiltà* Cattolica 125 (1973/II), pp. 367–75. For a complete list of the publication of documents of the ITC, see chapter 7 of this text: also M. Flick, "Pluralismo teologico e unità della fede, in: *La Civiltà Cattolica* 121 (1970/I), pp. 323–33, which we are following here in the main outline of ideas.

30. *Dei Verbum*, n. 19.

31. Rousselot, "La grâce d'après S. Jean et S. Paul," in: *Recherches de Science Religieuse* 18 (1928), pp. 87–104.

32. Cf. Gross, *La divinisation du chrétien d'après les Pères grecs* (Paris, 1938).

33. Cf., e.g., J. Chene, *La théologie de Saint Augustin* (Le Puy, 1961); St. Augustine, *De Perfectione iustitiae hominis*, c. 3, *PL* 44, 295.

34. Cf. *Syllabus* of Pius IX, e.g., DS 2980.

35. Cf. Leo XIII's action in favor of Thomism, e.g., DS 3155.

36. Cf. Pius X's documents, DS 3401–3500.

37. The encyclical *Humani generis*, DS 3875–3899.

38. *Gaudium et spes*, n. 43.

39. Cf. the example, far from exemplary, of the Franciscan Girolamo di Montefortino (d. about 1728), who set forth the doctrine of Scotus in the order of the *Summa Theologica* of St. Thomas.

40. Document of the International Theological Commission (ITC) on the *Unity of Faith and Theological Pluralism*, no. 1 in *Documentation Catholique*, no. 1632 (May 20, 1973) or *La Civiltà Cattolica* 125 (1973/II), pp. 367–75.

41. *Ad gentes*, n. 21–22; Vatican Council II, *Decree on the Church's Missionary Activity*, (December 7, 1965); *Gaudium et spes*, n. 62.

42. *Unitatis redintegratio*, n. 17.

43. *Unitatis redintegratio*, n. 4.

44. *Spiritual Exercises*, n. 22.

45. *Dei Verbum*, n. 8.

46. Cf., *Lumen gentium*, n. 25.

47. Cf. Gasser, *Mansi*, 52, 1213.

48. Document of the ITC *Unity of Faith and Theological Pluralism* no. 11, in: *La Civiltà Cattolica* 124 (1973/II), p. 369.

49. *Ibid.* n. 8.

50. Instructive reading in this connection are the personal memories of Fr. Lagrange, published by the Bible School of Jerusalem: *Le père Lagrange au service de la Bible* (Paris, 1967).

51. Document of the ITC *Unity of Faith and Theological Pluralism* no. 10.

52. Cf. Vatican Council I, *Constitution on the Catholic Faith* (DS 3011); *Lumen gentium*, n. 25.

53. On the norms governing dissent see: *Human Life in Our Day: A Collective Pastoral Letter of the American Hierarchy* (November 15, 1968).

54. Cf. in this connection Newman's deep considerations on the usefulness of the noninfallible Magisterium for the progress of theology, in chap. 5 of *Apologia pro vita sua*.

55. Cf. Z. Alszeghy and M. Flick *Il peccato originale* (Brescia, 1972), pp. 28–9; 319–24.

56. *Lumen gentium*, n. 25.

57. *Il messaggio della fede oggi*, Letter from the German Bishops to all those in the Church who have received the mandate to proclaim the message of faith, n. 18, It. trans. (Milan, 1967), pp. 17–18.

58. On the function of universities in the Church of today, cf. H. Carrier, *L'université entre l'engagement et la liberté* (Rome, 1972), pp. 18–22; 143–89, 236–240.

6

Theology and Life

A frequent subject of Marxist thought is the connection between philosophy and praxis. Not infrequently there is opposed to the classic model of philosophical cognition (in which truth is a mental representation of reality), the ideal according to which thought creatively forms the future reality projected.[1] Theological methodology, without of course renouncing realism, agrees with this postulate, because it sustains that the understanding of faith, if it is genuine, not only expresses what exists, but also transforms the thinking subject and thereby becomes leaven in the world. The acceptance of faith, according to St. Paul, is a chain reaction since the believer, changed interiorly by the Gospel, reflects its light and becomes a principle of conversion for others (cf. 2 Cor. 3: 18–4:6).

The great theological tradition had no difficulty in adopting this trend of theology toward orthopraxis. Theology, in fact, prolongs the intrinsic orientation of the word of God, which is destined to bring forth and develop life: "These are written that you may believe ... and that believing you may have life in his name" (John 20:31). For patristic antiquity it was evident that the methodical contemplation of the mysteries, in spite of its "theoretical" character, aims also at affective and practical assimilation of its object.[2] Medieval Scholastics arrived at the same conclusion, stressing that theory, the understanding of faith, participates in the dynamism characteristic of faith, which is acceptance of God the Savior.[3]

The stereotyped question whether theology is a theoretical or a practical science has sometimes been interpreted as if Scholastic theology had been divided about the interdependence between life (spiritual and active) and cognition (theological). This is a misunderstanding. The discussion refers only to the "immediacy" of the subordination of science to action; that "sacred science" appeals to the whole of human existence was never questioned.[4] Therefore, medieval morality always distinguishes between the rightful desire for theological knowledge and "curiosity."[5]

Only the influence of the nineteenth-century concept of "science without preconceptions" sometimes made theologians forget the existential aspect of their own doctrine. Today the most frequent accusation against theology is precisely that of being abstract, alienated from life, detached from Christian experience, and not interested in building up the Body of Christ. There are, in fact, a good many priests who declare that they have found in theology an obstacle rather than a help for their spiritual life, and who affirm that the store of knowledge, acquired by means of the institutional courses in seminaries or universities, is of no use for their priestly ministry.

These comments are so widespread that they have led more than once to the attempt to construct, alongside classical theology, another theology, intended to interpret the Christian kerygma as a call to animate Christian and community existence, taking into account the present situation. If, since the Council, the division of theology into two sciences does not exert a stronger attraction, it is because we recognize how deeply all theology is bound up with holiness and with the personal and communitarian action of its subject.[6]

In these pages, our concern is not that of judging the value of present-day theology (defending it or condemning it), but rather trying to determine what is the right path for the theology of tomorrow.

Theology and Christian Existence

"To be a Christian," of course, does not consist only in that real and ontic newness realized in the baptized infant, who, according to the faith of the Church, becomes a member of the Mystical Body of Christ, the temple of the Holy Spirit, adorned with sanctifying grace. But Christian existence cannot be identified either with personal data (that is, the fact of being registered among the members of a religious association), nor can it be reduced to a cultural fact (being formed in the intellectual and institutional traditions of a society geared to values appreciated by the Christian message), nor to an ethical fact (accepting in practice, or at least in theory, certain rules of behavior).

All these elements are integral parts of one reality, germinally present in the child, supremely developed in the saint. It is a question of an orientation of the whole set of forms of behavior, internal and external, individual and communitarian, postulated and produced through contact with the Christian mystery, accepted personally (intellectually and affectively) as truth and value. Christian tradition has classified this type of existence into themes, applying the schema of the three "theological virtues": Christian existence is, according to the description of a well-known manual, "a moving in a divine and not a human way in the whole of reality, by means of *charity* in all its dimensions, *faith* in all its perspectives and *hope* in all its phases. This is the total object of theological life: God before anything, but also creatures in their place."[7]

We must avoid the rather frequent misunderstanding of thinking that this "Christian existence" is a purely individual phenomenon, which has arisen from the meeting of an individual person with a book. For a "living faith" (complex of theological life), a language suited to expressing the mysteries is necessary, and a message proclaimed in this language is necessary ("How are they to believe in him of whom they have never heard?": Rom. 10:14). And the concrete experience of the value of human attitudes, through testimony, is necessary, and incorporation into the community, through which spontaneous attitudes can be "legitimized" on the plane of reflection, is necessary. All that is not the work of the individual, but the community, the life of which, even before it is scientifically explained, must be "interiorized" by the individual.[8]

But for an intense life of faith, it is also necessary that intellectual and affective acceptance of the mystery not only should be the result of a process of socialization, but should also correspond at least to a minimum extent to a religious experience. "Experience" in this context means "a feeling, a perception, with which the absolute is reached not only through images, concepts, ideas..., but also by means of an immediate impression of the presence of the Absolute and through man's response which integrates this impression."[9] For the most part such a perception is not a meeting detached from the listening to the message, nor does it give in itself new contents independent of the message, but rather it is a deep dimension of the listening itself, as a result of which, the object to which the message refers is imposed on the mind as a personal reality of dialogue and attracts affectivity, spontaneous and decisive, as a value.

The Christian believes that to have this experience "the grace of God and the interior help of the Holy Spirit must precede and assist, moving the heart and turning it to God, opening the eyes of the mind, and giving "joy and ease to everyone in assenting to the truth and believing it."[10] It is a question, therefore, of a direct influence of God in the believing subject, which is carried out normally within the community of believers, as a result of which the subject is incorpo-

rated more intensely in it. This influence mainly remains an uncon-
scious one, and its reality is testified in the necessity of prayer and
thanksgiving for one's own faith.

The Christian also believes that this experience, although being a
free gift of God, which is realized without presupposing merits on the
part of the one who receives it, does not remain, at least for a long
time, without the "fruit" of corresponding attitudes, communitarian
and individual, intellectual and affective, internal and external,
which have found concrete expression in the classic triad: prayer, austerity of life, love and oblation for one's neighbor. "Good works" not
only condition the arising and continuation of living faith, but also
are its natural expression: through them the experience of faith is
reinserted in the community context.

Christian Existence — The Condition of Theological Activity

In our "lexicographical approach," speaking of "theology as an
activity of faith" and a "science of faith," we already pointed out that
theological study *presupposes,* as a necessary conditioning for the
theologian, a spiritual and existential context characterized by the
thological virtues.[11]

In all sciences, a practically indispensable condition of fruitful research is prescientific experienced with regard to the object of research. As a result of which, the findings, in spite of their abstract
limitedness, are understood as part of the complex reality. Everyone
admits the precariousness of purely bookish knowledge; one can
hardly become a doctor without some contact with clinical reality, nor
can one engage in sociology without having participated in a community life. If one has no religious experience, one can learn what is
necessary for a theological examination, one can explain also various
theological terms, but one cannot "engage in theology," that is, one
cannot arrive at discovering through formulas the meaning of the
mysteries, in their analogy with empirical reality, in their connection
with one another, and with the ultimate purpose of human life.[12]

It is possible to illustrate the necessity of a deep spiritual life for
the success of theological study, in the light of observations made on
"genius," which disposes toward success in scientific research. A
scholar, who lacks even the slightest degree of "genius" for research,
can work wonders of patient and persevering application but will
never succeed in obtaining notable results. Scientific "genius" is intellectual openness to given aspects of reality, a "dim presentiment of

the truth," in which solutions are grasped intuitively even before they have been proved, a creativeness with which one has the desire and the capacity to replace conventional formulations with other original ones, a flair for understanding structures through particular elements, for discovering the meaning through phenomena, for catching a glimpse of functional relations through the succession of facts.

In theology, for great achievements it is necessary to have that particular attitude described by classical theology[13] as the set of gifts of the Holy Spirit. It is surprising how similar are the intellectual attitudes the great masters of Catholic tradition consider as fruits of the gift of wisdom, of the intellect, of good judgment, of knowledge, to the forms of behavior psychology describes as the manifestations of "genius." It is a question of a force by which "one is led" to seek and to find the understanding of faith by means of the various ways of theological reflection, as a result of which one grasps intuitively, beyond formulas, truth; in reality, value, in the part, the whole. Such an outstanding natural and supernatural disposition is not actually acquired, but its presence is normally bound up with a community environment of living faith, and is united with a generous and prompt readiness to face even a painful purification through courageous action and physical and moral sufferings.

One of the causes of the poverty of theology today is the fact that stress is rarely laid on the importance of creativeness, originality, boldness in research, since these gifts, which are indispensable for the development of a science, are sometimes considered incompatible with faithfulness to the norms of theological study. This mentality is partly responsible for the attraction of the opposite extremism, and also explains why little emphasis is laid on the action of the Spirit in theological study, as if the Spirit operated only through institutions.

The necessity of a considerably developed theological life for the success of theological study was seen in the past by the importance given to "saints" in theological argumentation, owing to the fact that the Christian sense of the faithful was included among the "theological focal points"[14] in the category of connaturality with the supernatural mystery. It was supposed that those who are more closely united with Christ have the "sense of Christ," that is, a better capacity of judging the truth of assertions regarding the mystery of salvation (1 Cor. 2:72–16). This persuasion was studied a great deal in the category of the "supernatural formal object" of faith.

Theology is an intellectual activity, which is the connatural prolongation of faith; therefore it can be realized under the same conditions that are necessary for faith. Faith is a supernatural act, which is possible only when the intellect considers its object in a light, in a horizon, different from that of natural knowledge, characteristic of the human intellect. Otherwise, man would not be capable of grasping in human words a divine invitation to enter into a personal communion with God, which is inconceivable on the basis of empirical experience alone. The doctrine on the necessity of grace for faith (and for that prolongation of faith, which is theology) also implies the necessity of theological life lived personally, since the gifts can transform personal life only when they are freely accepted.

The importance of Christian life for theological research is particularly clear in the so-called argument of suitability. We have shown elsewhere the very great importance that this argument had, e.g., in the Marian dogmas of 1854 and of 1950, and recently in the theology of development and liberation, which (like all the theology of the "genitive of object") implies an intuition of what God thinks on the basis of what he has told us about himself.

The reflections indicated here help us to understand why a good many people consider theological studies useless for the progress of their own Christian lives, and even harmful for an incisive priestly ministry. It is mainly a question of cases in which theology has been confused with accumulated factual knowledge, or prolonged controversies on formulas, outside the climate of spiritual experience, an experience to which the two Vatican Councils refer when they speak of the sweetness of assenting to the truth and believing it.[15] Such a pseudotheology, based on purely factual knowledge, animated not by the sentiment of worship but by contestation of the manifestations of the religious sense, averse to "pietas,"[16] filled, on the contrary, with the "bitter jealousy" described in a way that is perennially topical in the letter of James (3:14), is in fact, really harmful, since it creates the illusion of knowing the mysteries, whereas it plays merely with their empty skin.

Theological Activity—Nourishment of Christian Existence

The historical fact that the great spiritual movements (monasticism in southern Gaul after the fall of the Roman Empire and monastic renewal of the eleventh and twelfth centuries, the Franciscan and Dominican evangelism of the thirteenth century, the Catholic reform of the period of the Council of Trent), produced a theology of their own, makes us think. Persons concerned about their own spiritual life and that of others experience the fact that contemplation is emptied if it is not *nourished* by thoughts developed also on the intellectual plane. That applies today more than ever, since as Voillaume rightly notes, "in the present circumstances it is not possible to maintain a high level of Christian life without a degree of religious knowledge superior to what was necessary when there was a united Christendom."[17]

This is not to say that theological study leads directly and by itself to comtemplation; at certain moments, temporarily, one has the impression that it rather dries up prayer. Christian existence, in its vital unity, is all the more stimulated by the reality of the mysteries, the more concretely and vividly they are presented as values and as appeals to personal acceptance. That interpretation of ecclesial life, which is theology, does not offer new realities for contemplation; the object of theological discourse (creation, incarnation, redemption, real presence, eternal life), is known to us from childhood. Theological study alone does not bring the mysteries nearer to us. On the contrary, it may give the impression of increasing the distance, since it expresses the message of faith, self-implicative, symbolical, and capable of being experienced, in the language of science, which is factual, verifiable, and therefore abstract. The poetic description of a spring may fill us with nostalgia but the chemical analysis of its waters leaves us cold.

Yet all true theology (even the driest) is useful for Christian life, since, in the first place, it offers prayer wider and more certain themes. It is true that contemplation is an intuitive and affectionate knowledge of the mystery but, after a certain time, it is emptied if it does not find new elements. Points of view that once strongly impressed us become stale with habit. Theological reflection calls attention to new aspects of the mystery, which contemplation then develops and deepens. The relationship between theological reflection and contemplation can be compared with the relationship that exists, according to St. Thomas,[18] between teacher and disciple. The teacher cannot make things evident but can call attention to aspects of reality that the intellect understands. In the same way, theological science offers material in order that contemplation can apply itself to keen cognition of its object.

In the second place, theological science *guides* Christian life, indicating the experiences and positions (interior and exterior) that should be characteristic of the real disciple of Christ. To know that I should repent, give thanks, admire, forgive, commit myself for my neighbor, does not replace or infallibly produce these forms of behavior; but it is an appeal, a stimulus, an orientation for Christian life.

Finally, theological science *verifies* spontaneous experience. The anguish of mystics, who often fear they are deceiving themselves in following what seems to them an invitation from God, the concerns of spiritual directors who doubt to what extent they can encourage or approve the way of acting of those they counsel, are a countercheck of the usefulness of theology, which unmasks illusions, completes exclusivenesses, and checks exaggerations.

In particular, theology exercises an indispensable function in the *transmission* and legitimization of Christian life.

The Christian community must continually *initiate* new members to its life. These are unlikely to be able to interiorize the persuasions and appreciations that constitute the background to the behavior demanded by the Church, unless the message of salvation is set forth to them also in a conceptual and orderly way, showing clearly the relationship of the attitudes suggested with the normative sources of faith.

Furthermore, in the *continuation* of Christian life, new problems, also intellectual ones, arise, not least of all because of the contact the believer has (and must have) with his or her own environment. The Christian community lives in actual fact in an atheistic society in which membership of the Church is at least tacitly but continually challenged. It is not possible to legitimize one's life without a minimum degree of rationalization of the spontaneous and intuitive adherence to Christianity.

Following the practice of the patristic Church, the liturgical apostolate of today distinguishes carefully the various phases of the progressive "socialization" through which the believer assimilates that community life of salvation that is Christianity: the precatechumenate, the catechumenate, and mystagogy.[19] All three stages imply a progressive exposition of faith, which not only is theoretical, but also calls for a theology to nourish it. This necessity explains why the "didascalos," the "teachers of the sacred page," were considered from the most ancient times useful members of the ecclesial community. As St. Bonaventure pointed out, their work imposes silence on adversaries, sustains the weak, and delights the perfect.[20]

Making Theology Come Alive

Although every true theology corresponds in some way to the postulates just described, the vital function of the Sacred Doctrine can be emphasized more or less, helping (or hindering) the influence of orthodoxy on orthopraxy. The *vitalization* of theology certainly does not consist in renunciation of intellectual precision or in use of a sermonizing style, but rather in *stressing the point at which theological questions spring from praxis,* and the point at which they *lead to real life experience.*

The starting point of great theological controversies has nearly always been a question raised by real life. The Christological and trinitarian problems of the first four centuries were caused by perplexity regarding how to reconcile worship of Christ the Pantocrator with the confident and obedient adherence to the Father, which is a constant in the life of Jesus. Pelagian polemics arose in the spiritual circles of fourth-century Rome in which the effort was being made to renew Christian commitment in the tired atmosphere of a Christianity that had become the state religion; the subtle semi-Pelagian discussions were inevitable developments of a qualm of conscience agitating the monks of Adrumeto and Marselles. The Lutheran reform would have been unthinkable without the painful search to find with certainty a propitious God, and Jansenism was the rigid rationalization of the great spiritual experience of Port-Royal.[21]

These historical crises of Christianity do not belong exclusively to the past, but are of perennial interest, because they are phenomena that constantly accompany the Christian experience. They existed mosted germinally, before the doctrinal controversies broke out and, in a certain way, they continue to lie in wait along the spiritual path of individuals. One can hardly live Christianity intensely without their coming to one's consciousness sooner or later. At a certain phase of one's spiritual development, each one is tempted by Monophysitism, or by Nestorianism, by Pelagianism, or by Jansenism. The latent crises of orthodoxy are all the more dangerous the less one knows the guidelines that the community of salvation has taken once and for all, under the influence of the Holy Spirit, with those self-implying definitions that progressively construct the nature of Catholicism. Therefore in the study of any dogmatic assertion, the first step must be to identify and in a certain sense relive the spiritual experience that gave rise to the controversies, and to discover under the historical masks a perennial spiritual drama of Christian life.

A second way to vitalize theology consists in considering *the impact of the doctrine on one's own spiritual attitudes.* Although this point of contact is mostly discovered by understanding intuitively how a doctrine changes the horizon of personal existence (an intuition unlikely to be had outside the framework of prayer, charity toward one's neighbor, and austerity of life), it can be brought about, however, by asking oneself, for example, the question, "What would change in my life if I took really seriously the single elements of the Christian message or, on the contrary, if it were proved that this or that element is false?"

Those who are deeply convinced, for example, that they are led by an almighty goodness, that they are destined to survival after physical death, that humanity is marked by original sin, and that Christ is alive and operating through the institutional reality of the Church, have an unmistakable stamp on the whole of their lives, a stamp the beauty of which is perhaps the strongest argument for the credibility of Christianity (Cf. 2 Cor. 2:14–16). Then, too, we do not even realize how deeply Christian principles influence the judgments of value that, even if unconsciously, direct our lives; If the fundamental dogmas of Christianity were false, we would not have any reason to condemn forms of behavior from which our moral sense spontaneously shrinks.

These points of contact between orthodoxy and orthopraxis emerge with surprising clarity in ecclesiastical history (real history, which does not limit itself merely to recording external facts), in which it is seen how effective the truths of faith were in the construction of the personal lives of the saints and in the creation and development of communities that lived their faith intensely.

Theology and Construction of the Church

Revelation was communicated to men so that they might form a community of believers, the new people of God, called to worship God in community life, in spirit and in truth, offering the sacrifice of their own filial life in union with Christ's sacrifice. The study of theology, being a development of revelation, would have no meaning, therefore, if it were not subordinated to the construction of these people, the temple of the Spirit, formed of living stones.

The connection between theological study and the construction of the Church does not consist just in that relationship that every scientific study has with the construction of humanity, and therefore with the glory of God. To limit the vital efficacy of theology just to nourishing the individual Christian existence of the theologian, would be a contradiction of the spirit of Christ's message, which was communicated as a light not to be hidden under a bushel, but to be placed on a candleholder to illuminate the whole house.

The connection between theology and the communitarian construction of the Church seems clear when it is shown that theology cannot develop fruitfully without contact with pastoral action, and that pastoral action cannot do without theology.

Pastoral Interest — The Condition of a Good Theology

The necessity for theology to have a pastoral dimension is verified by history. Those few theological movements that took no interest in pastoral action, are known as deplorable examples of a reflection that, though it may have been subtle, was barren. Although the theology of the Fathers was a reflection of the pastors of the Church in proclaiming and defending the faith, although monastic theology was laid down as a spiritual nourishment for the monastic community, and although the great Scholastics of the Dominicans and the Franciscans came into being as a preparation for popular preaching, nominalism was, perhaps, the first great intellectual movement in the Church that was concentrated on speculation on the mysteries. Isolated from the interests of the community, it was guided not only by the needs of the Church, but by the internal impulse of the intellect to develop certain subjects to the point of absurdity. The theology of the Counter Reformation was again an action of the whole Church, not only as a reaction against the Reformation, but also as renewal of Christian life; think of the theology of the Jesuits in the seventeenth century and of St. Alphonsus Liguori.

Nineteenth-century theology was characterized, on the other hand, by a certain detachment from pastoral requirements, both in its Neo-Scholastic form and in its attempts to adapt itself to the culture of the time, as for example in semirationalism and fideism. The "apastoral" nature of this theology was manifested also in the dogmatic Constitution *Dei Filius* of Vatican Council I, which, in a certain sense, spoke over the heads of the faithful on problems discussed only in university lecture rooms. For this reason alone, it did not bring about a theological renewal comparable with the fermentation that followed the first five ecumenical councils, the Council of Trent or Vatican II.

The coincidence between pastoral interest and theological depth can be explained in the light of what we said regarding *the starting point of theology*. Theological reflection presupposes an *ecclesial life*, which seeks understanding of its cultural-linguistic nature. This life becomes the object of experience and makes its demands felt particularly when the Church is building herself up — in missionary preaching, in homiletic instruction, in catechesis, in the creation of liturgical prayer, in the emergence of institutional forms, and in the dialogue between the community and the environment. In the self-construction of the Church, community life is revealed as reality and value to such an extent as to justify the effort to give it an intellectual interpretation, that is, to construct a theology. In the very act of self-construction of the Church, problems, which the scholar at a desk would not, perhaps, have discovered, become urgent. On the other hand, purely technical questions, which may worry the isolated thinker, but the solution to which has no influence on the life of the community, lose importance.

A second explanation of the connection between pastoral interest and theological depth is based on the fact that *the sense of the reality of the mysteries,* to which the message of salvation refers, is found more easily in the self-construction of the Church. In individual study, one is more easily tempted to reduce to algebraic signs, the terms referring to supernatural reality, so that reasoning proceeds through the combination of these signs, as with the dynamism of a calculating machine, without the thinker's remembering what these signs mean.

We are thinking of problems such as the following: if Adam had not sinned, would children have had the use of their limbs from the beginning? If a divine person had become incarnate in a lion, would the latter have kept its ferocious nature? What does a mouse eat when it gnaws the consecrated host? Similar "problems," discussed seriously in learned disputes, show how the automatism of formal thought proceeds when it loses contact with the realities of the things signified and lets itself be submerged by that "metaphysical delirium," which the French theologian Henri de Lubac stigmatized in the history of the "second Scholastics."

The self-construction of the Church, on the contrary, in which it is necessary to announce and explain realities and values that have an influence on the real lives of persons who are not always intellectually developed, forces the thinker to return to the reality itself, to the "thing," and to discover again and again the concrete meaning of the formulas.

The paradoxical affirmation of one of the pioneers of the present liturgico-catechetical renewal is often quoted: to solve operational problems, there is nothing more practical than a good theory.

Reflecting on this sentence, we think of those great mass movements, which are changing the face of our world. All of them, without exception, constructed, right from the beginning, an ideology as an indispensable instrument for their duration and expansion. The wide interest aroused by the publication of Rosenberg's *Myth of the Twentieth Century,* the perseverance with which members of the Communist Party study and comment on the difficult and dry works of Marx, Engels, and Lenin, the fanaticism of the young, waving Mao's red book as a greeting — all call our attention to the necessary function of a doctrine in creating a lasting community that requires sacrifices of its members, and that show how erroneous is a narrow pragmatism that throws itself into action without having reflected on its meaning.

In spiritual renewal movements of the Church, in which the announcement of the Word has a determinant influence, the leaders of these movements often rely right from the beginning on a theological elaboration of the message, and if sometimes an initial mistrust of a science too abstract or developed in too autocratic a manner brings about a certain anti-intellectual attitude in them, they subsequently have recourse to it in order to nourish their own charismatic zeal and that of their followers. Theological reflection plays a significant part in the work of the great preachers, not only in the patristic age, in which the homily was still a literary genre of theological research, but even later, when the separation between science and diffusion in theology was completed. St. Bernardino of Siena, St. Vincent Ferrer, and St. Vincent de Paul felt the necessity of a reflection not only on the mysteries, but also on the function of the preacher with regard to the effective proclamation of the faith. In our times, the crisis of preaching has even led to the development of a new branch of theological research, "the theology of preaching."[22]

On the other hand, conversion movements that remained deliberately adoctrinal — for example, Frank Buchman's Moral Rearmament — in spite of sincere good will and the considerable means used intelligently, led merely to a temporary reawakening, and their followers kept their effects only to the extent to which they became integrated in other movements with better doctrinal foundations. Nor can it be otherwise.

Faith, the foundation and root of Christian existence, "is not a vague cry," but a deliberate adherence to God through Christ, as a result of which one accepts the message as revealed by God (and therefore true), and one accepts the ecclesial community as willed by

God (and therefore good). Fundamental Christian experience implies, therefore, the acceptance of a reality that in the etymological sense is "instituted" by an Other, and is therefore "institutional." If we think that the mystical experience (in prayer and action sacrificing itself for charity) goes beyond all conceptual representation, it must not be concluded that it is not rooted in worship or in religious teaching.

The Christian mystics of contemplation and praxis rise to God starting from a message and a rule of life. The ecstasy, it is true, surpasses any clear and distinct idea, enthralls and transports the soul, but when it ends, the subject is again plunged into the circuit of conceptual representations and forms of behavior chosen according to their conformity with ideals or with norms. The ecstasy itself is recognized in the latter, it is expressed through the latter, and it relies on the latter to direct itself and to take flight again. The spontaneity of the intuitive experience not only does not prove anything against the theoretical doctrine and against the practical regulation but, on the contrary, requires them as its source and its result.

In order that all the heritage of doctrines and laws may be possessed by the multitude in a lasting way, the community must reflect, pick out common elements from the variety of experiences, compare them, organize them, verify them, express them in ever new intellectual schemata, and apply them in the solution of problems emerging from ever new historical contexts. In other words, the community of salvation was and is able to spread beyond the barrier of centuries and cultural territories only to the extent to which it continually rethought and rethinks the eternal gospel in a series of various ideal systems. All this can be carried out only with a "scientific" activity, which, of course, is not limited to being only scientific. Therefore limitation to pure pragmatism that claims to do without scientific reflection is a perennial but disastrous temptation for the apostolate.

This conclusion, the fruit of a theological reflection on Christian experience, is also seen from a sociological consideration of ecclesiastical life. The Church, in fact, as a visible community, is subject to the laws of sociology. It is an absurdity to expect that there should be a community movement extended throughout the whole of mankind and destined to last for all time, without a certain "socialization," that is, without the "typifying" of experiences, facts, and persons, without the constitution of "roles," and without an effort of "legitimization," showing that the structures have a meaning, based on objective truths, and have a normative force derived from values and laws that are absolutely valid. All that continually implies a complex intellectual activity. Experts revealed from the flux of community life the fixed system of truths and values that supports it (a "symbolic universe"). On the basis of this system, they establish the "therapy" (through which sufficiently intelligible and convincing motivations are offered in order that members who are tempted or who have strayed may be strengthened or may return to the framework of community life) and a "prescription" (to destroy the strength of motivations that might lead to deviation from this framework). All this is carried out to a certain extent also in a spontaneous, preconscious, and occasional way but, especially at moments of crisis or conflict, the critical and systematic objectification of these procedures, that is, what we normally call a scientific reflection, is inevitable.

We have tried to show clearly the requirements of the life of the institutionalized group in order to prove that if one wants to proceed with the construction of that mysterious reality, the appearance of which is described in the New Testament, and the destinies of which are studied in ecclesiastical history, by applying the procedures proposed by pastoral theology, it is not possible to do away with the science of faith, that is, theology.

Making Theology More Pastoral

Let us avoid a radical misunderstanding. The postulate of putting theology in the service of the community does not mean that theology should be *carried on in an assembly*, in such a way that everyone — atheists and believing Catholics, uneducated persons, and specialists — should seek the understanding of faith together, chorally.

As the German theologian, Cardinal Joseph Ratzinger rightly pointed out in an interview, "the opinion that the formulation of Christian faith should be as clear to the man in the street as the language of advertising posters, is a glaring mistake."[23] It is a mistake to demand that the liturgy and the homily should be in a language that is immediately understandably also to the "distant." As Ratzinger rightly observed in his interview, "modern linguistics has proved clearly that, when all is said and done, there does not exist a language understandable to everyone." There is a common heritage of words, but their meaning is not completely fixed but is determined also by the historical, sociological, and psychological context in which they are used, that is by the linguistic play. Although they speak the same tongue, sportsmen, hunters, technicians, and artists express themselves in different languages, so the same word may

have very different meanings in the various vital and dialogical contexts, and a sentence, composed of words known to everyone, may
become incomprehensible outside the linguistic play in which it was
uttered. The creation of such a jargon is not always the result of affec-
tion but corresponds to the need to express without interminable cir-
cumlocutions mental contents common to a group of persons, but unknown to outsiders.

It is natural, therefore, that the community of those who live in
the light of Christ's mystery, as it is revealed in the Bible and was
developed by tradition, should have their particular language; otherwise they could never express the specific daily experiences of their
community existence. For example, community doxology would become silent if it had to renounce speaking about the mysteries.

The mysteries of salvation are designated with words that, outside the ecclesial linguistic play, have no meaning or have a different
meaning: Trinity, Word, Son, Spirit, Incarnation, inspiration, state of
grace, sacrament. Man cannot make (at least in a community way) his
self-giving to God without using in creative and self-implying formulas words taken from the description of human interpersonal relations, changing considerably the meaning of those words. We are
thinking of terms such as lordship, service, fatherhood, filiation, covenant, wedding, dwelling-place, and merit. The community language must not, of course, arrive at a Hermetism that repels outsiders,
but outsiders penetrate the language at the same rate as they penetrate the real life of the community, since they learn to speak of the
realities they believe and eventually may experience.

It is equally natural that those believers who have made a labori-
ous and extensive analysis of the contents and foundations of ecclesial experience, should in their turn use a conventional language,
which is different from the one spoken by the other members of the
community of salvation.

That is particularly evident when it is a question of determining
the relationship of faith with an ideology or a theory that already has
a technical language. Valid, communicable, and controllable reflections in these questions are not possible in a language comprehensible to all because the very terms of the comparison are formulated
always and only in a specialized language, just to express a complex
thought exactly and precisely.

But even when it is a question of reflections strictly internal to
the message of faith, these reflections will have to use a language
that makes it possible to reduce thought to standardized, studied, and

tested forms. The expert, listening to an address, recognizes the problems, the facts, and the theories to which the speaker appeals, and the procedures that are used.

For example, following an explanation on original sin, the listener realizes that the author began with the exegesis of Rom. 5:12 according to the exegete Anders Nygren, continues it by using the figure of the "argumentum ad hominem," as C. H. Dodd did, touches on the Council of Trent, using the hermeneutical principle proposed by Haag. If the one offering the explanation had had to explain every step of the reasoning, the address would have become interminable, and the listener's attention would have been dispersed in a thousand details, without the possibility of understanding and judging the meaning and the value of the theory proposed.

However, if we insist that a theology useful for the edification of the Church sometimes demands the use of a technical language actually understandable only to specialists, we do not think at all that discussions among theologians should deliberately be kept concealed (as if for a new application of "disciplina arcani") from nonbelievers and nonspecialists. The suggestion is often made that theologians should discuss their theories behind closed doors, under the guarantee of close secrecy, in order not to disturb the peace of the "good Christian people." Only when they arrive at real certainties could they propose their conclusions in public. Such a procedure is impossible, and it would end up by being even more harmful than the ambiguities and perplexities feared.

In the situation brought about by the development of the media of social communication, in the light of the demand of the public to be informed, it is very unlikely that prolonged and an extensive discussion among theologians, on a question of a certain importance in the Church, could be kept secret. A refusal to give information about the discussion would give free course to irresponsible leaks, which would distort the opinions proposed far more without the possibility of rectification.

But even if it were possible to stop all leaks, the result would be harmful. In the first place, the results of a discussion, held behind closed doors, would cause a real scandal if communicated suddenly to the ecclesial community. It would, in fact, be incomprehensible why, up to that point a certain way of teaching had been followed, while from then on it was necessary to embrace another opinion and adopt new practices. An answer is comprehensible only if the preceding questions are thoroughly understood and felt. A willing acceptance of teachings and directives cannot take place unless people know the path along which these positions were reached. Then, too, it is absurd to claim that nonspecialists should wait passively until specialists solve the present day problems of Christianity. The public can wait for archeologists to find the meaning of the Etruscan language because this problem has no impact on everyday life, and can be solved without the help of the public. The problems of faith concern every Christian. While the specialists are discussing behind closed doors, the nonspecialists would inevitably be driven to discuss among themselves in front of the doors. In this way two parallel theologies would be produced, both incomplete and asphyxiated: a science of mandarins, without the impulses and correctives of community experience, and a pseudoscience produced by incompetent people, which is incapable of discovering its own contradictions.

Between a tumultuous "choral theology" and an aseptic "laboratory theology" lies the "community theology," which is related to the building-up of the Church through the directions it receives from her, the applications it offers to her, and the group environment in which it works.

1. There will be a contact between the dynamic life of the Church, which is continually building up, and theological research, if research takes its *orientation* from the questions *actively* emerging from pastoral life.

At the beginning of our reflection, we indicated that ecclesial life is the starting point of theology. But that must not be understood as if ecclesial life should be only the passive object of theological research. The community fact fully becomes a starting point for research, if study takes from that life the impulse and the direction of the attempt at interpretation; in other words, if the theologians try to understand ecclesial reality in terms of the living reality that drives toward self-understanding.

The orientation thus described takes place when the theologians themselves take part in the dynamics of pastoral life, participate in the need to clarify ideas, solve problems, develop impulses received, in order to pray together more consciously and to be able to explain the message better to others.

This necessity seems to be particularly felt in American theological circles today. On the one hand, the subjects with which American theologians began their research were very often suggested in international centers by teachers with little knowledge of American life, or even by foreign publications alien to the problems of the Church in the United States. On the other hand, there was a widespread opinion that the hierarchy provides for the needs, even the intellectual ones, of the Church, asking, if necessary, for information from some specialists. In this way, and also as a result of the cultural isolation of seminaries, theological thought has been little stimulated by pastoral life. Greater attention to the questions emerging "from the rank and file," as, in fact, is already observed in various theological reviews and above all in teaching in various seminaries, will give greater impetus to studies and research, and above all will help American theology to find its own place in the international theological movement.

2. A truly communitarian theology aims at applying the results of research to the building-up of the Church, that is, to the deepening and extension of ecclesial communion. When a theologian, having studied a problem, does not feel any impulse to use the result of this work to teach, to console, to admonish, or to encourage, either the study was not sufficiently geared to the mystery, or his pastoral activity lacks doctrinal sensitivity. In fact, theology is a science in that it sets forth the message of Christ in all its dimensions; and the Christian message contains essentially an "economy" aspect, that is, a functionality that aims at moving the individual person and the community of believers toward salvation.

A very concrete and practical way of finding the application to the intensive and extensive development of the ecclesial community (that is, to the apostolate), is to ask oneself at every stage of theological research the three questions: (a) How could I explain this doctrine to a simple person, in the environment in which I live (to a child, to an old person)? In fact, beyond technical formulations, clear formulas to say what is essential. (b) What difficulty would a critical mind living in my environment (the doctor, a worker who reads a great deal) meet with on listening to the exposition of this doctrine? One understands the doctrine when one divines also the difficulties to which it gives rise, to be integrated in the cultural background. (c) What would have to change in my enviornment (in the liturgy, practices of piety, in morals) if this doctrine were false?

A practical opportunity to put the result of one's studies, even specialized ones, at the disposal of the community is offered by renewal courses, given for the clergy in pastoral care, and for other lay groups, Bible circles, etc., which meet to deepen their knowledge of the word of God.

3. The orientations received in pastoral life and the applications

made to pastoral life may, however, remain elements extraneous to the research itself, a kind of plaster put on over the wall. There is the danger that the impulse received from community life is only an external occasion of study, and the application of an artificial corollary.

In the last decade, an attempt has been made to offset this drawback, especially in the United States and in Germany, by approaching theological research as the joint work of an interdisciplinary group, carried out, that is, by persons with various specializations who, meeting in prayer, in active service of their neighbor, and in study, seek the formulation of the word of God corresponding to the present requirements of the community.

Such a group constitutes a meeting point between the individual thinker and the whole people. It is utopian, in fact, to demand that the scholar should be continually immersed in the life of the masses; this would not permit qualified work, which has determined requirements regarding the environment, instruments of work, concentration, etc. The interdisciplinary group, on the other hand, produces a dynamic movement, effective and possible, in that the thought is not formulated definitively by an individual and subsequently adapted to others, but comes into being right from the beginning in the group dynamics, that is, in the dialogic tension of the various points of view. The group, supposing, of course, that it is not an occasional gathering, but one with a real reciprocal opening of minds, becomes something more than a mere addition of the parts. It is kind of vital space, a dynamic field, which influences the individuals and ensures that their research will be entirely structured according to the service requirements of the whole community.

In this field only the first steps have been taken, exploring how to overcome difficulties also of a practical nature; but we feel that, by our proceeding in this direction, initiatives will be reached that will produce abundant fruit in the future.

The Cultural Ideal

The connection between science and life is a basic problem common to all disciplines. In the training of doctors, teachers, etc., discussions similar to the ones familiar to theologians are carried on because, on the one hand, pure research in laboratories and archives has no influence on the life of the masses and, on the other hand, normal professional service (medical, scholastic, etc.) becomes inefficient when it is isolated from the progress of researches.

The attempts by law faculties to solve this problem reminds us that a solution of the problem "science and life" (in our case, "theology and life") comes into focus when the aim is not limited to producing through science results useful for society, but when scientific formation is geared to an ideal, which is organically integrated in the culture of the society itself and accepted as a value by society. In other words, science and society must be understood in the perspective of the role that society attributes to a person who is fully educated.

The history of Western civilization knows various cultural ideals that have followed one another in giving their stamp to various phases of culture, and therefore also to scientific studies.

The Aristocratic Ideal

The cultural ideal of Greco-Roman antiquity is that of the free man, of the perfectly developed person (kalós kai agathós). From the intellectual standpoint, this ideal is incarnated in the "sage," who, just because of his right way of reasoning, is also virtuous. The way to become such is constituted by "enkyklios paideia," that is, by the harmonious ensemble of the liberal arts,[24] which, in their organic and measured complexity, are often compared to a choir. It would be a defect against balance if a free man wished to penetrate one of them too much, to the point of "acribia," in detail. The particulars, the practical applications, can be left to slaves; the important thing is that through general culture the person becomes wise and, as such, capable of directing others.

This ideal, conceived by Greece and inherited by Rome, emerged repeatedly even later in the flux of cultural history. Its variants, applied to the times, appear, for example, in humanism, in the college system at Oxford and Cambridge, in the period at the end of the nineteenth and the beginning of the twentieth centuries in the university seminars of Germany, in the colleges of higher education in France and in Italy, in which science seemed the apex of the development of the universal spirit.

It is not surprising if the community of believers shared esteem for this cultural ideal. The "true gnostic," the contemplative, was considered until the Middle Ages the eye of the Mystical Body, the member that directs the movement of the arms that struggle (the knights) and of the feet that walk (the working people). Esteem for complete and harmonious knowledge inspired the monastic conception of "contemplata tradere" and the cultural ideal represented by the image of the shell, which fills with the wisdom coming from above, while the abundance of its content overflows upon others.

In this context, the connection between theology and life was ensured by the full spiritual development of the theologian. Being imbued with a methodical contemplation of the Christian mystery, he would be a guide for others toward the goal he already knew. One can understand in this way why in the twelfth and thirteenth centuries a teacher at Paris University was considered the ideal candidate for the episcopate, so much so that the title "magister" could designate both the teacher of theology and the head of a group of preachers.[25]

The Bourgeois Ideal

Western civilization always knew the figure of the specialist, an official of society with specific duties.

In antiquity, the "expert" had a clearly subordinate position. He could be a useful instrument under the guidance of a freer mind, as a specialist in the trades, in the "mechanical arts" (among which disciplines as important as medicine or architecture were sometimes included), or as a slave teacher, who instructs future leaders.

Later, the importance of specialists grew. In the modern age, the center of culture has become the university, maintained by the state; and the state directs this costly institution not to the formation of a privileged élite, but to that of good officials in the administration of justice, in public health, in teaching, later also in commerce and industry. The importance of university faculties changes. Theology loses its hegemony (and often also its place among the other faculties); the importance that philosophy had in the nineteenth-century university has passed to philology, and even more to the natural sciences necessary for the development of industry. The cultural ideal of the bourgeois age is the expert useful for society, and he or she is incarnated in the scientist or artist (at the higher level) and in the doctor, teacher, accountant, etc. (at the lower level), who possesses an updated professional training to offer society highly qualified services.

It is very significant that this tendency, apparently a secular one, was manifested in ecclesiastical studies first. The early Middle Ages introduced the monastic and capitular schools above all else with a view to providing dignified liturgical celebration, and for the sake of preaching. The *Institutio clericorum* of Rabano Mauro[26] was directed almost exclusively to this ideal. The reforms of Trent directed at the formation of the clergy subordinated studies to the formation of good pastors of souls. In this framework, the connection between theology and life was aimed mainly at a knowledge of the dogmatic assertions that the faithful had to believe, and of the moral norms they had to observe. From the beginning of the twentieth century, more and more importance was gradually given to "apologetics" as a preparation for the future pastor ready to rebut the objections of the incredulous. It was just the practical and professional tendency to solve given questions that encouraged the splitting-up of theological teaching into various disciplines, and specialization in research.

The caricature type of criticism that is made today of teaching in the seminaries before the Council, is certainly often unjust. Where the system was fully developed, it contributed a great deal to the acclimatization of theology in the cultural life of the respective nations (we are thinking of the theology faculty at Tubingen and Munich or of the Catholic Institute in Paris). Where development was delayed, the people's life of faith often lacked the necessary intellectual substructures. But the system belongs to the past, not because of its internal deficiencies but because of the decline of the cultural ideal incarnate in it, that of the official specialized in religion.

The Ideal of Socialized Culture

The role that present-day society assigns to its members who have reached perfect development in intellectual formation, is no longer that of teacher (sage or official) in front of ignorant disciples. In the age of advanced socialization in which we live, such a relationship is felt as being degrading for the multitude, which is perceived as the real protagonist of cultural progress. The cultural ideal, in this context, is not that of power used with regard to the group (albeit in favor of the group); it is not a knowledge posessed by one, of which others are deprived, but the capacity of living and seeking together with everyone. It is a question of a service, which the individual member renders the community by means of his or her own specialization, and by stimulating community researches, by offering documentation and material for discussions, pointing out the value of the results. Perfect cultural development, therefore, does not produce leaders who push or drag society along, but specialized organs, which express and coordinate the mass movement.

The life of the Church always undergoes the influence of the way in which the society in which she lives, develops and understands it-

self. There is no doubt, therefore, that also in the present circumstances a deep restructuring of ecclesiastical community life is immi-
nent.[27] In the framework of this transformation, there will change also
the figure of the theologian, that is, of the one who, within the community of salvation, is specialized in interpreting critically the life of
the community. In theology, the new way of integrating the specialist
in existential and community life is workable, more than in any other
discipline. In fact, the expert in profane sciences knows many things
that the other members do not even imagine.

The theologian, on the other hand, must always keep in mind the
possibility that in his environment there are persons who, owing to a
greater maturation of their Christian personality, penetrate the message of salvation beyond what the rationalizing procedures of science
can express. Sometimes the theologian himself will have the impression that, welcoming generously the word of God in the community,
he himself divines in his heart depths that science cannot grasp. The
memory of the ignorant old woman to whom St. Bonaventure ap-
pealed[28] is always able to deflate the theologian's professional pride.

As Karl Rahner points out in volume nine of his *Theological Investigations*, it is not easy to determine what are in particular the
practical and operational postulates of the new cultural idea in connection with the integration of theology in the life of the Church and
of human society, especially because they vary according to the different cultural areas. In the next chapter, dealing with theological di-
dactics, we will mention some. In our opinion, on the level of content,
the new approach does not add anything essential to what we have
set forth in this chapter on the connection between theology and life.
It clarifies, however, the *nature of the necessity* to vitalize theological
science and make it more pastoral.

In the cultural environment of the aristocratic or bourgeois ideal
of science, the union of theology with spiritual life and with the apostolate may have seemed an accidental element added to pure science
from outside; in fact, the utilization of the science of faith for individual and community orthopraxis may have been considered a
humiliation of pure science. We have repeatedly stressed that such a
connection is postulated by the *message of salvation,* the subject of
theology. We can add that in the framework of socialized culture this
connection appears as postulated also by the very nature of *science,*
produced by the community, with the forms of thought specifically
characteristic of that community, with the purpose of developing the
total life of the community.

The ideas expressed in this chapter, dedicated to the connection between theology and life, are crystallized in the sentence of the Gospel of John: "If you continue in my word, you are truly my disciples, and you will know the truth, and the truth will make you free" (John 8:32).

We know very well that the "truth" of which St. John speaks is far more than a set of theological assertions. It is a question of the luminous reality of God, communicating itself to men in Christ Jesus. "To know" this truth is not only science but also fullness of life. But, if the evangelist presents the meeting with divine reality as introduced by an existential attitude (to continue in the word) and in a certain sense a community one (to become one of the disciples), and leading to an existential attitude (to be freed from the slavery of sin), we, too, will do well to think of our theology (far more than was done in the immediate past), in the existential and community context of Christian life and of the building-up of the Church.

CHAPTER NOTES

1. Cf. Cornelio Fabro, *God in Exile Modern Atheism* (New York, 1968) pp. 672–735; Vincent Miceli, *The Gods of Atheism* (New Rochelle, 1971), pp. 92–142.

2. This applies also to Alexandrine Christian gnosis itself: cf. W. Völker, *Das Vollkommenheitsideal des Origenes* (Tübingen, 1931), pp. 76–144.

3. Cf. Bonaventure, 1 *Sent.* Proem. q. 3 (Op. 1, 13).

4. Cf. Thomas Aquinas *S. Th. I*, q. 1, a. 4 (in which St. Thomas affirms that the sacred doctrine implies both the practical aspect and the theoretical one, but rather "magis" the theoretical one).

5. Hugh of St. Victor, *Didascalia*, 1, 5, c. 10 (*PL* 176, 798); *S.Th.*, II-II, q. 167, a. 1.

6. Cf., e.g., C. Colombo, "Teologia ed evangelizzazione," in *Scritti teologici* (Venegono Inferiore, 1966), pp. 151–74; H. U. v. Balthasar, "Theology and Holiness," in: *Verbum Caro* (Einsiedeln, 1960); K. Rahner, "Consideration on the Development of Dogma," in: *Theological Investigations*, Vol. 4 (New York, 1974).

7. G. Thils, *Christian Holiness* (Tielt/Belgium, 1961). quoted in Italian from the 2nd edition Italian translation *Santità cristiana* (Alba, 1969), p. 726.

8. Cf. P. Berger, *The Sacred Canopy* (Garden City, 1967), *The Precarious Vision* (Garden City, 1967); T. Luckmann, *The Invisible Religion* (New York, 1967). The original text makes reference to P. Berger, T. Luckmann, *La realtà come costruzione sociale* (Bologna, 1969).

9. W. Thuhlar, *Lessico di Spiritualità* (Brescia, 1973), p. 220.

10. *Dei Verbum*, n. 5

11. This is an unquestioned axiom in theological tradition. Cf. St. Bonaventure (*Itinerarium mentis in Deum*, Prol. n. 4: Op. 5, Quaracchi 1891, 296), quoted in the Vatican Council II (*Optatam totius*, n. 16, n. 32): "Nemo credat quod sibi sufficiat lectio sine unctione, speculatio sine devotione, investigatio sine admiratione, circumspectio sine exsultatione, industria sine pietate, scientia sine caritate, intelligentia sine humilitate, studium absque divina gratia, speculum absque sapientia divinitus inspirata" (trans. Let no one think he will find sufficiency in a reading which lacks unction, an enquiry which lacks devotion, a search which arouses no wonder, a survey without enthusiasm, industry without piety, knowledge without love, intelligence without humility, application without grace, contemplation without wisdom inspired by God).

12. We understand "engaging in theology" as the acquisition of that "very fruitful understanding" that Vatican Council I considers possible for one who "sedulo, pie et sobrie [zealously, piously and soberly]" seeks it "tum ex eorum quae naturaliter cognoscit analogia, tum in mysteriorum nexu inter se, et cum fine hominis ultimo [not only from the analogy of those things which it knows naturally, but also from the connection of the mysteries among themselves and with the last end of man]" (DS 3016).

13. Cf., e.g., E. Ranwez, *Les dons du Saint-Esprit* (Liège, 1945); L. M. Martinez, *The Sanctifier* (Paterson, N.J., 1957).

14. Let us point out that, as a result of reflection on the development of the Marian dogmas, the importance of the "sensus fidelium" has regained its topicality. Cf., e.g., C. Dillenschneider, *Le sens de la foi le progrès dogmatique du mystère marial* (Rome, 1954), and its value was reaffirmed by Vatican Council II. *Dei Verbum*, no. 8, includes among the factors of dogmatic progress "the intimate understanding of spiritual things".

15. DS 3010; *Dei Verbum*, n. 5.

16. DS 3016.

17. R. Voillaume, *Sulle strade del Mondo*, Ital. trans. (Brescia, 1960), p. 137, note 7; Cf. R. Voillaume, *Source of Life, Eucharist and Christian Living* (London, 1975).

18. *De veritate* q. 11 a. 1–2; *Ibid.*, q. 9 a. 1; *Ibid.* q. 22 a. 8–9; *S.Th.*, II-II q. 6 a. 1; *Super Mt.* c. 23 1. 1; *Super Joh.* c. 5 1. 5.

19. *Ordo initiationis christianae adultorum* (Vatican City, 1972) For a complete English text of this rite see: *The Rites of the Catholic Church*, (New York, 1976), pp. 13–181).

20. St. Bonaventure, 1 *Sent.* Proemium q. 2 (Op. 1, 10–11).

21. Port-Royal. French site of a woman's abbey founded in 1204 near Paris. Its nuns were originally Benedictine, and later, Cistercian. In the seventeenth century it became a center of Jansenism and was destroyed.

22. Z. Alszeghy, M. Flick, "Il problema teologico della predicazione," in: *Gregorianum* 40 (1959), pp. 671–744; D. Grasso, *Proclaiming God's Message* (Notre Dame, 1965).

23. From the magazine *Settimana del clero,* issue of November 1, 1973, p. 4.

24. It should be remembered that the organization of the trivium (grammar, rhetroic, dialectics) and of the quadrivium (arithmetic, music, geometry, astronomy), beginning with classical antiquity, throughout the Middle Ages up to the Renaissance, remained the basis, even the institutional basis, of secondary education.

25. Cf. M.D. Chenu, *Nature, Man, and Society in the Twelfth Century* (Chicago, 1968).

26. *De clericorum institutione* 1. 3; c. 1, *PL,* 107, 377.

27. With regard to the image of the future Church, we refer readers to K. Rahner, *The Church after the Council* (New York, 1966), *The Shape of the Church to Come* (New York, 1974).

28. L. Lemmens, *S. Bonaventura* (Milan, 1921) p. 211.

7

The Study of Theology

The question, how should theology be studied, is apparently a very personal one. Its place would seem to be more in the context of a confidential conversation between a disciple and a master than in a book. At least in the past, in fact, it was raised only by a few, who were looking for a way suited to their own capacities, inclinations, and duties, in the objective and unshakable framework of the system.

Now, in the present theological situation, the question presents itself differently. It has gradually become a problem of the whole Church.

In the first place, there has been an increase in the number of persons who need directives in their studies. Those who enter a seminary no longer feel they are entrusted to the mechanism of a great institution, which takes them as on a conveyor belt to a desired end. On one hand, the pluralism accepted by the institution calls for individuals to plan and choose between various possible programs; on the other hand the crisis of the institution challenges them to question the fixed framework of these programs.

And it is not only young candidates for teaching or for the priesthood who pose the question of how to study theology. It is often after the conclusion of the normal course of studies that the priest discovers both the necessity of deepening, updating, and continuing his own studies to meet the new requirements emerging from the pastoral ministry, and his lack of preparation in planning study personally. Above all, there are an ever-increasing number of the laity who feel the imperious necessity of bringing their religious culture into line with their level of intellectual maturity in order to be able to carry out that mission of apostolate demanded by their condition as adult Christians.[1]

There are theological schools in which most of the students are lay people, and specialized institutions for the theological formation of the laity are multiplying. These laity, obviously, often feel confused at the threshold to theological studies, which were conceived in the past almost exclusively in relation to the preparation for the clergy, and therefore they are particularly in need of practical methodological guidance.

But today there is another reason why the question of how to study theology is an ecclesial problem. To become a theologian is no longer an exclusively individual matter, like becoming a philologist or an expert in history. Here it is a question of assuming a new role in the life of the Church, with new tasks, requirements, and therefore rights. The sociologist would say that to study theology implies a "secondary socialization" in ecclesial life. An individual can enter his new capacity as a specialized theologian only if the community meets him halfway and offers him not only institutional means (teaching, library, etc.), but above all encouragement and understanding. One of the causes of the crisis of seminaries themselves is that bishops and the faithful in the Church often do not understand sufficiently the value and the conditions of a thorough theological formation. Therefore, all Catholics need to realize what are the suitable procedures for studying theology.

We are speaking of *various* procedures. In fact the concept still quite widespread in the immediate period after World War II, that one becomes a theologian by reading carefully a given number of manuals or by listening to different courses of lectures for a certain time, providing finally by means of an examination that one has assimilated their content, is anything but traditional. In the great period when theology flourished, formation was obtained by means of a complex structure of various didactic exercises, which completed one another. Perhaps the most complete didactic system was that of Paris University, at the time of St. Thomas. The two daily lectures (one biblical, the other systematic), the ordinary disputations repeated several times a month, the two annual quodlibet disputations, the university sermons (or rather theological meditations) on feast days, personal meditative reading, progressively increasing participation in the master's teaching after obtaining the bachelor's degree, and literary activity for the preparation of one's own comment on the sentences, formed a many-sided, harmonious unity, at once flexible and severely demanding. Our attempts today, after all, try to replace this organism (the atrophied remains of which constituted the framework of theological formation until very recent times) with a new one, corresponding to the requirements of theological work today. It is always, however, a question of an organism containing various elements, in which one element has a meaning only in the whole formed by the entire structure, to such an extent that the disorder, hypertrophy, or elimination of one of them, calls for a corresponding change in all the others.

The Magisterial Lecture

According to a students' bulletin, the stress laid on the importance of magisterial lectures causes one to suspect that the invention of printing has passed unobserved. We are quite aware of the fact that printed books exist. We think, however, that, for a complete and effective formation in any field, but especially in theology, the magisterial lecture is a means that, though not sufficient by itself, can hardly be replaced by others.

Of course, there may be magisterial lectures that, for lack of preparation or owing to the absence of pedagogical gifts in the teacher, and also because of the low cultural level and lack of application on the part of the audience, could be suppressed without loss, just as there are books that are not worth reading and research groups that break up without having achieved anything. It is not possible to attribute to any didactic exercise an efficacy "ex opere operato," and it is a mistake to compare the didactic contribution of a poor lecture with that of an excellent book, read under optimal conditions. A didactic system must set up the various institutional forms of teaching, expecting an average performance, without being able to exclude the possibility that one or another of the didactic exercises planned may, for particular reasons, function imperfectly. The president of the rectors of German universities pointed out with realistic bonhomie that as, unfortunately, in every institution, so in academic teaching is it necessary to reckon with a certain quantity of stupidity and maliciousness.[2]

It is often said that the most advanced institutions of higher studies eliminated some time ago the preponderance of magisterial lectures. This is not correct. The universities of the European continent, which are certainly not inferior to the others (except, perhaps, in the purely technical field), and which are, in any case, more suited to the mentality of the average European, continue to base their teaching on magisterial lectures. Attempts to create a radically different didactic system have not obtained satisfactory results up to now.

It is true that in the Anglo-Saxon world universities with a minimum number of magisterial lectures operate most successfully (Oxford, Cambridge, Harvard). But to judge the phenomenon, we must remember that the success obtained is limited to determined fields of knowledge (e.g., classical philology, sociology, psychology). Moreover, these universities admit a severely selected student body, they have excellent equipment (e.g., reading rooms with many copies of the same works), and an exceptional staff (specialized "tutors," free of nonscientific commitments, in the proportion of one for every ten students). Therefore the didactic system of these universities cannot be transferred to other universities that are not so well equipped. In fact, not all British universities follow the Oxford system; far less do the theological faculties and seminaries of other countries, where the sociological, financial, and organizational substructures are essentially different.

The appeal to the practice of others does not dispense us, of course, from the obligation of setting forth the reasons for which we believe in the usefulness of the "magisterial lectures."

The first reason refers to the communication of *notions*. Certainly, it is not a question of handing down to the student through the magisterial lecture the "wisdom of the ancients," understood as a treasure of notions and rules acquired once and for all (which could also be done by means of a book). Today the ideal of science (and therefore of teaching) is not to preserve a fullness already obtained in the past but to seek progress in the future. Therefore the main aim of teaching is to bring the students to a fully developed intellectual life, to make them learn behavior, operational schemata, an ethics of scientific thought, the "rules of the game," so that the new generations can enter that community dialogue that continually renews the Church through "ongoing reflection."

But the "formal" elements of study remain without foundation, without knowledge of "material" elements, that is, of the results and methods accepted by the cultural environment today. Magellan certainly had the makings of a brilliant navigator, but if he were to return to the earth, he would be incapable of carrying out the task of a master mariner, owing to his ignorance of facts, procedures, and instruments. Even the most brilliant theologian needs notions verified and formulated precisely (e.g., he must know how knowledge of the literature of the ancient East contributes to the interpretation of the inspired texts), a method of work (it is not possible to study theology with profit today without taking hermeneutical requirements into consideration), familiarity with scientific aids (one cannot proceed in theology without being accustomed to consult the normal sources of information, such as dictionaries, bibliographical lists, etc.). The lecture helps the students not to lose their way in the immense multitude of informational data and opinions, which they meet with at the beginning of specialized theological studies, and which, even in the Middle Ages, seemed to the "novice" a dark forest full of obstacles.[3]

This is obtained in all sciences in that the teacher divides the vast field, which constitutes the subject of a determined study, into parts, picks out from the multitude of phenomena relatively constant groups of facts as samples (pattern), and stresses the structure uniting the plurality of the elements. In dogmatic theology, by means of a similar procedure, the teacher not only gathers from the sources (biblical, patristic, conciliar) what refers to a given question, but also shows examples from exegetic, patrological, historical, and speculative literature, which indicate how the sources must be interpreted, and how an implicit solution of the problems that emerge from the contemporary situation of the Church can be derived from their explicit teaching. The didactic usefulness of this procedure can be seen by reading a medieval biblical commentary, which, referring to a text, mentions numerous dogmatic and moral questions, so that the systematic doctrine must be gathered from various explanations.[4]

Naturally, the division, classification, and structuring of the material can also be carried out by means of publications, and are therefore found in manuals. But what books can never do adequately is adapt these didactic processes to the student's present horizon, determined by his general culture, the point he has reached in the course of theological study, and the daily experiences that influence the mentality of the group. When the lecturer sets forth a doctrine, even unconsciously he plays upon the points of contact through which the doctrine answers questions already existing in the minds of listeners. He appeals to the aspects under which the content of the teaching has already entered the intellectual world of the student. He polemicizes with the misunderstandings he observes and emphasizes the aspects through which the subject of the teaching can normally arouse interest.

The students rarely manage to appreciate this work of adaptation of the doctrine because their attention is concentrated on the content, and they know only the doctrine already adapted.

Following the teaching of our former pupils, we find not infrequently that their audience judges as original and brilliant those who expound strange doctrines, which are often also uncertain and useless, whereas the lesson of those who try to make understandable a substantial doctrine, indispensable for the understanding of faith, is considered a mere reading of the manual. Only later do students realize the usefulness of the teaching received, sometimes thinking that they had found by themselves what was the result of a good teaching method.

However the purpose of the lesson is not just to communicate a *doctrine*. The help that the lesson gives to form a *synthesis* is very important. We have already pointed out that the synthesis is not an element added to the analysis but a knowledge of the details, as a result of which one notes their mutual relationship and their connection with the central element constituting the heart of a problem. Even the assiduous reader of different publications will only rarely succeed in discovering by himself the organic unity of the various studies, the complementarity of the problems, the convergence of results, in such a way as to understand some central theme more deeply. It is the magisterial lecture that calls the listener's attention to the synthetic unity of the various doctrines.

Finally, the principal value of the lesson is not only that it proposes thoughts, but also that the audience sees the thinker himself as he approaches truth. In various ways, which are often unconsious (with the voice, with gestures, with the total attitude, with marginal remarks), a methodology and a spirituality lived by the theologian are communicated, that is, just those values most postulated by the contestation of students who desert the magisterial lecture, are transmitted. It is an illusion to think that methodology can be learned in abstract, without applications to the contents. Methodology codifies topical schemata, legitimizes procedures, but does not cause the practice itself to be learned. Seeing someone else reason, one learns how to pose questions, how to interpret the sources, how to use instruments. The students are enriched, even if they do not accept their teacher's method. Often a new form of thought is found, congenial to the mind of the subject and to the nature of the object, in dialectical reaction to another model of thinking. The refusal of a model may be necessary to find another one, just as for a jump one must lean more intensely, for a moment, on the platform one wishes to abandon.

That all this is not just abstract theory but experienced reality can be seen by reading notes taken during the lectures of brilliant teachers. The oral lesson had filled the audience with enthusiasm, but the recording without the visual dimension, and even more the transcription deprived also of the acoustic dimension, become colorless, insipid, unable to arouse interest.

The lack of magisterial lectures is one of the main obstacles to the formation of lay theologians, who are very often prevented by their specific study and by the exercise of their profession from attending regular courses on theology. This lack can be made good to some extent by means of evening classes or gatherings that last for a few days, in which expert teachers deal with some particular points, initiating students also into group work, and answering the questions that emerge from the discussions of the groups.

Lessons, such as the ones described here, cannot be improvised. A remote preparation, even a thorough one, is not sufficient, not even if the subject matter has already been taught repeatedly. Although many individual factors must be taken into account, it can be said that, for a good academic lesson, at least two hours of immediate preparation are necessary, one to collect the material and another to set it out.

It is generally useful to take a textbook as the basis of the lessons. This saves a lot of useless work, both for the audience and for the lecturer. It is, in fact, a mistake to think that it is almost an obligation to a lecturer, right from the beginning of his career, to present a reflection on the whole structure of the treatise entrusted to him. The teacher's attitude with regard to the manual must neither be one of slavish dependence nor one of systematically destructive criticism.

The teacher's task will be, on the one hand, synthetic (to highlight the dynamism of the thought), and on the other hand analytical (to deepen and complete the phenomenology of images, themes, and concepts, to interpret the individual sources exegetically and speculatively, to drive home the relationship between the lived experience and the conceptual reflection). It will be very useful also to suggest paths for personal work so that the students may be stimulated and guided.

It is generally unnecessary for the lecturer to write the whole text of the lesson. This takes up too much time and may tie the lecturer down by preventing him from changing his exposition in a cybernetic way according to the impulses he receives from the audience. The most useful way of preparing lessons seems to be to rewrite, before every lesson, an ample, clear and orderly schema, which one can then keep in front of himself or herself while speaking to the audience freely. Even more important is an intense preparation of all the movements of thought, so that the subject matter is experienced in its unity and therefore in its communicability.

Intense and extensive preparation is not possible when the

teacher is weighed down with lessons and also has to carry out other activities (teaching in public schools, systematic pastoral care in the parish, etc.). The teacher will be fully occupied with a maximum of twelve lectures on theology a week. A seminary that imposes more work on its teachers institutionally excludes the proper functioning of the institution.

The magisterial lecture has all its usefulness only when it becomes the guiding thread of personal study on the part of the student, who prepares it, assimilates it, and completes it. Experience shows that lessons are wasted when the student cannot dedicate at least as much time to master the material proposed as the length of the lesson. Considering that the time of students of theology is occupied also by several other activities (preparation for the priestly ministry, study of languages, sports, etc.), the ideal number of weekly lessons seems to amount to about fifteen; twenty constitutes a limit, which cannot be passed with impunity, without sacrificing the seriousness of personal reelaboration.[5]

Group Study

Group work corresponds to a postulate of pedagogical psychology today, and it has become necessary in the academic organization of theological studies because the students, accustomed from childhood to active pedagogical methods, could not adapt themselves to the role of an isolated and purely receptive subject. But it would be a mistake to consider active and community cooperation in teaching as if it were an alien element imposed from outside. Actually, the didactic system of theology, worked out in the second half of the thirteenth century, corresponded in a high degree to the requirements of group dynamism. The organization of the medieval university, with the wise balance of the various powers and the various corporations, with the participation of individuals in discussions with roles that were progressively and qualitatively different, was a masterpiece of active community dynamism.[6]

The "second Scholasticism" of the seventeenth century continued at least a part of this tradition. The historian of theology after the Council of Trent is often struck by the facility with which former pupils of the "Roman College," on returning to their countries, succeeded in taking their place in the various philosophical and theological problems that were found there, presenting a documentation well adapted to a concrete approach, with a logical structure of thought.

This outstanding capacity of maneuvering with the information received at the time of studies was one of the excellent fruits of the ancient "Ratio studiorum," in which the students were required to rethink actively (alone and in a group) the subject matter of the "prelessons," "objecting to themselves and solving their own objections." To stimulate and direct the activity of students, the various colleges had their "coaches," teachers who had the task of getting students to repeat the subject matter with a view to examinations, as the name might suggest. But these teachers were also directors of private studies and animators of the "circles," groups in which the students of a college discussed, generally twice a week, the subjects of the lectures. The Roman College incorporated this work in the "sabbatine," (Saturday disputations) and in the "monthly" or extraordinary disputations held with greater solemnity.

In the nineteenth century the manner of operation of these groups hardened, losing all spontaneity. On the other hand, especially in the modernist crisis, the syllogistic form lost its meaning because the real problems referred to the interpretation of the sources, and therefore preceded the syllogistic reasoning that presupposes assertions that are clearly formulated conceptually. But with the elimination of the disputations, a gap was produced in the didactic system, which evidently had to be filled. The students who came out of the ecclesiastical schools were in conditions of inferiority as compared with those who had been initiated in the lay universities in personal research, especially in the philogical and historical field.

In 1931, the Constitution "Deus scientiarum Dominus" tried to remedy this drawback, adopting in the ecclesiastical universities the exercises corresponding to university "seminars." This reform certainly brought advantages, but it was not enough to stimulate the personal and community activity of students because the "seminar," originally conceived as a small group for the best students, was not very effective in any discipline to move a student not endowed with a marked scientific interest, and also because the "exercise" often lay outside theological teaching.

After World War II, efforts were resumed all over the world to revive the dynamics of the student group. This time the model for the new initiatives came from a very difficult cultural environment, that is, from the technique of political and cultural conferences, held in the United States, to influence public opinion. Up to now, the adaptation of the new forms to academic teaching, especially in the field of theology, cannot be said to be a complete success. There are many reasons for this. One is the fact that, after the first experiences, which are attractive owing to their novelty, systematic active participation calls for an effort that neither teachers nor students have the strength to impose on themselves when the institutional system does not demand it; and the institution, in a period in which priestly vocations have dropped considerably, dare not establish new obligations. In spite of this, the didactic necessity is stimulating attempts all over the world to introduce these forms, and the fate of theological teaching is bound up with their success.

Here is a set of samples of the initiatives most in use today, arranged according to the extent of personal preparation demanded from students. We begin, therefore, with those active and community teaching methods that can be carried out without specific personal preparation, gradually proceeding toward those models in which the real work shifts more and more to prior preparation, so that the pooling of results can be considered almost a spontaneous development of the work done.[7]

Dialogue Lesson

The simplest form of active student participation in the lesson occurs when they have the opportunity to intervene with questions, objections, or supplementary remarks, and the teacher answers or (better) calls upon the other students to answer. Sometime the lesson may be interrupted by such a dialogue between teacher and students; sometimes the teacher poses some questions at the beginning of the lesson, and the students are asked to answer them; the lesson itself starts from these answers. A particular form of the dialogue lesson is one in which the teacher proposes a problem at the beginning of the lesson, and the students requested to work out the answer during the lesson; at the end of the lesson, the students' answers will be set forth and discussed. If the audience is a small one, the "circular consultation" method can be applied, in which each of those present is asked to express his opinion in the order in which he is seated. This method may stimulate even those who would not dare (or would not make the effort) to take part in the discussion of their own accord.

Six Times Six

When it is difficult to start the active participation of an audience that is quite large but not yet responsive, it may be useful to divide it

into groups of six persons. After a community consultation of six minutes on a question precisely formulated previously, the spokesmen of
the groups set forth the answers, which give an opportunity for a
clarification by the teacher or for a further general discussion.

The Specialized Group

The two methods just mentioned do not presuppose any specific
preparation on the part of the participants. In the specialized-group
methods, at least some members of the audience must already be
prepared beforehand.

In the "symposium" four or five students set forth as many aspects of a theological problem. The individuals speak for ten to fifteen minutes each. When the exposition is ended, the other listeners
ask questions, and the individual members of the group answer, each
for that part of the subject he has prepared. Finally, the teacher
gathers the conclusions and gives a judgment on the work done.

In theology, the traditional "theses" can provide material for such
an exercise. For example, with regard to original sin, one student
gathers the biblical foundations, another explains the thought of a
given Greek Father, a third sets forth the development of Augustinian
thought, a fourth comments on the fifth session of the Council of
Trent, a fifth interprets the thought of a contemporary theologian on
the subject, or makes pastoral reflections on the recent rite of the baptism of children. A more demanding version of the "symposium" consists of concentrating on the interpretation of a given document.

For example, to understand the canon of Vatican Council I on the
purpose of creation (DS 3025), one student sets forth the stands that
emerge from the work in preparation of the Council;[8] a second comments on the first phase of the genesis of the dogmatic constitution;[9]
a third sets forth the history of the new schema dated March 1,
1870;[10] a fourth determines the meaning and the dogmatic value of
the definitive text. To facilitate the participation of everyone in the
discussion, it would be useful to distribute a copy of the most important documents. Let us note that the method can be adapted also to
the discussion of the various chapters of a book, and can thus constitute an excellent preparation for the careful and critical reading of
scientific works. In this case, all the participants should have a copy
of the book.

The "round table" is merely a form of the symposium, which is
livelier, but also more difficult to prepare. The students represent dif-

ferent points of view concerning a theological problem that is debated. Each member of the specialized group sets forth briefly (for not
more than five minutes) an initial stand, and then, when all the others
have spoken, each one speaks again, even repeatedly, discussing in
front of the others, for about an hour. In a second phase of the exercise, the other persons present, who are not specifically prepared, can
also intervene, bringing forth clarifications or new discussions among
the members of the specialized group. For the success of the initiative, it is necessary for the main participants to agree on the main
lines according to which they wish to conduct the discussion.

This method can be used to present, or rather "represent" almost
dramatically, a subject of polemics in theological reviews today, e.g.,
the meaning of the liberation of the Christian, the real eucharistic
presence, the necessity of individual confession, etc. The round table
can lead to the understanding of deep discussions which it would be
difficult for a reader to appreciate rightly alone because it is difficult
to keep in mind the ebbs and flows of the opposite argumentations.

The Congress

The preparation of all the students is required for this exercise,
which, during a "study day," follows the method generally adopted in
scientific congresses. According to our experience, this exercise presupposes about a month's preparation, during which various groups
crystallize around a central theme, each geared to a different aspect
of the theme. On the morning of the day set aside for the "congress,"
the director of the exercise or a participant delivers for about half an
hour, a basic report that sets out the question. For two successive
hours, the participants divided into groups discuss the selected aspect
of the subject. The morning ends with a meeting of the spokesmen
chosen by the groups, who reach an agreement on the afternoon's
program, to avoid repetitions and establish a logical thread in the expositions.

In the afternoon there will be a general assembly, in which to
begin with, the spokesmen of the individual groups report the results
reached (each will need at least five minutes, but it will be more
satisfactory if they can speak for ten to fifteen minutes). Subsequently, after an hour's general discussion, the director of the day
will deliver a concluding speech, taking up a position on the content
and method of the discussions. The day may end with a eucharistic
celebration, with readings especially chosen by the participants.

The Seminar

The best-known but also the most difficult form of the students' active participation in theological teaching is the "seminar" or, as the "Deus scientiarum Dominus" called it, "the practical exercise." It differs from all the previous forms in that the student prepares not only to set forth in the discussion an opinion already known, but also tries to work out a personal opinion, and sets it forth not only orally but also in writing, in accordance with the practice of present-day theological literature.

The principal danger of this exercise is slipping into generic themes, which excite the beginner's imagination, but which he cannot elaborate sufficiently in the time at his disposal. These themes end up by being treated with clichés and rhetorical statements or at any rate ones that are not documented and proved. In this way, the seminar becomes a mere facade and does more harm than good because it accustoms students to an irresponsible, journalistic dilettantism. Therefore, it is necessary to stick to the principle that the subject suitable for a seminar is not that question to which the student wants to receive an answer, but the one he himself will be able to answer after six months' study.

A second danger is that each participant may work out an independent subject, in which case, the seminar lacks the group dynamism, which is indispensable for full intellectual development. To avoid this second danger, a precise general subject should be chosen, in which individuals can work out the parts of the whole. The coordination of the parts can be conceived in various ways. If the complete result of the seminar can be compared to a book written in cooperation by all the participants, a first model of cooperation is the "successive" one, in which each of the participants writes a chapter alone, and these contributions are set forth and discussed, one after the other.

A second model may be called "convergent": each participant studies an aspect or a source, and at each session of the seminar everyone contributes to clarifying a particular point.

In this second model it is often advisable to distinguish the subject of the oral report from that of the written work. For example, in the bisemestral seminar of the Gregorian University on the Augustinian definition of original sin, in the first semester each one sustained orally the theory of a modern historian regarding the interpretation of St. Augustine's thought on original sin; in the second semester, on the other hand, each one set forth in writing the concept of original sin as seen from a given work by St. Augustine.

It contributes greatly to the seriousness of the seminar if the written reports are kept and made accessible to all. If possible, at least the best works can be published in the year book, which can be sent also to former pupils of the institute and to other local academic institutes. Publications of this kind have not infrequently constituted the seed of periodicals destined to have a wider circulation.

We conclude our proposals on the active communitarian participation of students in the teaching with a few notes of a very practical nature.

The first one is that this cooperation may fail, not only because of the passive resistance of many, but also because of the excessive zeal of some unbalanced element who speaks too often or for too long, so that the others cannot or no longer want to intervene. To avoid this danger, the length of interventions should be fixed (and measured with a control clock), and no one should be allowed to speak for a second time until everyone has had the possibility of intervening once.

The second remark is that the figure of the group director can assume various basic styles. The "moderator," administrative or paternalistic, imposes programs, solves operational doubts, and therefore relegates the group to a purely executive role. The "animator" proposes programs, among which the group can choose, suggests various possibilities of work, with the respective motivations, which calls forth a sense of coresponsibility in the group. Finally, the "technical adviser" leaves the group alone, waits for it to appeal to him, and answers by offering only the information and advice requested.

The first style is sometimes necessary at the beginning, when the group is not yet really constituted; but as soon as possible a change should be made to the second style. The third style is possible only in the case, unfortunately a rare one, of a real leader emerging from the group itself, so that the teacher's role becomes rather an institutional covering for the spontaneous activity of the group.

In conclusion, let us point out that one of the reasons why stress should be laid in theological teaching on the introduction of active community cooperation is that it gives an opportunity to drive home community responsibility to the participants, so as to make them capable of cooperating with others, reaching decisions together with others, guiding others. In this sense, the active community cooperation of students through group dynamics is a real and proper means of professional formation and a selection test, as a result of which particularly the future priest becomes able to exercise one of the most important forms of the modern apostolate, that of the animator of spontaneous groups.

Private Study

At all times individual and prolonged reflection, by means of which the student endeavors to arrive at deep and at the same time critical understanding of the teaching received, has been considered one of the most important aspects of theological study. As the development of the terminology used in this connection shows, at the beginning individual theological study was not distinguished from contemplative penetration of the mysteries, and it was only in Scholasticism that it found intellectual forms of its own.[11] In the past, the positive doctrine that the theologian had to know was less extensive, on the one hand and, on the other hand, the magisterial lectures, which were more numerous, lightened the task of individual study in a certain sense.

At present, both the historical material (exegetic, patristic, etc.) and speculative requirements (the demands and the categories that modern culture imposes) have increased immensely, while lectures are reduced to the minimum, and the group work does not replace individual study but rather presupposes it by completing it. Therefore, the main problem of one who approaches the study of theology is how to ensure, organize, and perfect his own private study.

This concern is felt more or less keenly in all fields of cultural life. Therefore, there exists intelligent, penetrating works, written on the basis of thorough experience, which gather advice for students regarding the fundamental attitude to assume in order to cultivate one's own intellectual life harmoniously in connection with, for example, the art of reading and composing.[12] The reading of these works is also very useful for the theologian. Here we will merely add some specific applications, useful for theological study, especially dogmatics, taking into consideration above all the problems of those who are beginning this study.

We think that *three levels* must be distinguished in personal study: fundamental study, deeper study of given questions, and reading.

Fundamental Study

All further study presupposes knowledge of the ordinary teaching of the Christian message at present. In fact it is impossible to discuss a given question and look for new solutions until one has clearly understood the approach to the problem, the solutions already proposed by others, and the reasons why theologians have chosen a given explanation of the mystery.

It is essential that this fundamental study should not be limited to selected passages, but should be extended to the whole theological system. This is necessary for the deepening of the understanding of the faith. Most of the difficulties regarding the various theological theories do not come from contrary arguments, but rather from the incapacity of inserting an assertion organically in a consistent structure of intellectual interpretation of faith. The completeness of fundamental study is even more necessary for priestly preparation, since the "ministry of the word" cannot be limited to the announcement of "selected questions," but must proclaim the message of salvation in its entirety.

Since, generally speaking, teaching no longer gives a complete picture of the theological synthesis, theology students, for the most part, must turn to some manual that makes the classical doctrine accessible.[13]

It is important that, in private study, the student should work out the principal questions very schematically and in writing. In the choice of the main subjects to be prepared in this way, the examination program should be a guide.

In the written elaboration, it is very useful to follow the classic schema of "theses," which begins with the enunciation of an assertion, shows its connection with the preceding themes, explains the terms carefully, enumerates adversaries, and proposes the arguments on which the assertion is based. This schema, though decidely outdated as a research method, is very useful to gather and justify the results of the research. The existing compendiums can offer, in addition to the material, a structural model for this work, but they cannot replace it, since the personal elaboration of the individual theses is more important that its literary fruit.

The "explanation of the *terms*" must be done with that precision and clarity without which all scientific study is impossible, both in explaining the meaning of the problem and in proposing the solution. Although we know that our clear and distinct ideas never exhaust the mystery, since "the mystery of Christ ... goes beyond the possibilities of expression of any period of history, eluding for that very reason any exhaustive systematization,"[14] we must go beyond theological Cartesianism, not being content with confused, vague, or approximate ideas, but noting the inadequacy of the definitions worked out. It is impossible to do serious theological work without explaining what is meant exactly when terms such as creation, faith, justification, grace, merit, redemption, and sacrament, are used in a given context.

The traditional section dedicated to "adversaries" must not list Christians or even non-Christians who held opinions contrary to the "thesis," isolating them from their doctrinal context. The usefulness of becoming aware of "adversaries" is based on the fact that doctrinal development generally follows a dialectical line. When a problem arises from ecclesial life, the stand of orthodoxy is crystallized in opposition to some error; and when this stand is emphasized in an exaggerated and a one-sided way, and new change of orthodoxy moves away from this absolutization, giving new value to the grain of truth contained in the first error.

Let us think, for example, of the dialectical rhythm of Nestorianism, which led to Chalcedonian Christology, and of that of Pelagianism and Protestantism, which makes the teaching of the Council of Trent comprehensible. Therefore the enumeration of the main adversaires lends a proper historical setting or background to a dogma, as called for by Vatican Council II,[15] and serves to understand the meaning of the dogma more deeply, as a position of equilibrium in the eternal play of opposite extremisms. Another function of the recording of adversaries concerns ecumenism, which is recommended in the same section of the conciliar document. In fact, examining who are the real "adversaries" of a dogmatic assertion, one has an opportunity to reflect to what extent the theology of non-Catholic Churches and ecclesial communities differs from the faith of the Catholic Church.

The main function of the biblical, patristic, and magisterial "arguments," which must be gathered in the individual "theses," is not to "prove" the truth of the thesis, but rather to make intelligible in what sense there exists a continuity in dogmatic development. The biblical argument will not consist, therefore, of a list of verses in which the writer claims to find the assertion of the thesis or at least a premise of it. It will be a question rather of showing clearly, through the delineation of a biblical theme, the progress of revelation, which led to that dogmatic assertion that one is trying to understand.

The patristic and conciliar argument should abstain from quotations (perhaps learned by heart), which, especially if taken out of their context, do not have a real "probative" value. It is important, on the other hand, to know, citing some patristic work or some magisterial document, at what period, on the occasion of what facts, and in what form the Church realized that revelation implies the position expressed in the "thesis" in question, and to what extent the Church commits her authority for the validity of that formulation that appears in the thesis.

The speculative argument shows that the acceptance of certain formulations of faith postulates given intellectual positions in problems that arose later in the Church, so much so that a different solution would break the logical continuity of thought. Properly speaking, it will rarely be possible to fix these arguments in a syllogism, since the "middle term" is hardly ever univocally identical in the formulation of sources and in the solution of later problems. However, the syllogistic schema can become a very useful framework for the discipline of thought. The "major premise" may consist in the recording of a biblical theme, etc.; the "minor premise," on the other hand, may formulate the application of that theme to the question raised by the thesis.

For example, according to an argumentation proposed by Christ himself,[16] God reveals that he remains the God of his friends even after their death, that is, keeps his covenant relationship with them. This covenant implies that these friends of God survive after their death; therefore, God's faithfulness demands that those who lived as his friends on earth should survive death.

The recording of the principal "difficulties," and the principles in the light of which they can be solved, will complete the picture of the doctrine.

Deeper Study

During the first cycle of normal theological studies, the elaboration of the principal dogmatic assertions with the help of some good manual constitutes a task that does not *always* permit deeper study. It is highly desirable, however, that right from his first contacts with theological studies, the student should *sometimes* study more deeply *one or another aspect* of the doctrine, with the help of the common instruments of theological study. It does not seem impossible, in fact, that the student should dwell on some subject every fortnight, developing now the teaching of the Old Testament, now that of the New Testament, or the doctrine of some Father, of a Council, of some recent pontifical document, or even the speculative theory of some great theologian, ancient or modern. The rotation of these subjects, particularly in the first five-year period of ecclesiastical studies (philosophy and theology) will ensure that basic formation, complete and universal, without which the theologian never feels sure of himself. Together with the preparation of a "symposium," this deeper study will succeed in animating and stimulating group work, which is so important in modern scientific formation.

The usefulness of this deeper study is evident, not only for those who will have to promote theological research with teaching and with writings, but also for all those who dedicate themselves to the ministry of the word, in a society full of intellectual curiosity and marked by religious uncertainty. Anyone who is not accustomed to having recourse to the normal instruments for the verification of some theological affirmation, is at the mercy of all the theories, even irresponsible ones, that he comes across when reading the newspapers, and his proclamation can always be paralyzed with the formula dear to the incompetent, "today it is said...." At the same time, he will always be afraid of accepting theological opinions not contained in the manuals he used in his studies because he is unable to "test everything and hold fast to what is good" (1 Thess. 5:21).

In chapters 3 and 4 of this book, dealing with *"recourse to the past"* and *"opening to new situations,"* we indicated the main ways of this "further study."

To facilitate the elaboration of some question during studies (when the teacher has finished expounding a subject in his lectures, or when a session of the study group is being prepared), the seminary must have a "reading room" with the main reference works so that the ones most necessary for daily use are available in several copies for the students (at least one copy for every ten students). Such a reading room obviously does not dispense the priest from having these works for his personal use.

For a foundation in Sacred Scripture the student ought to have a good English translation of the Bible, the Greek text of the New Testament, a synopsis of the Gospels, a biblical dictionary, and a commentary on the New Testament. Following are some useful works in each of these categories, as well as some additional Scripture reference works:

The Holy Bible, Revised Standard Version, Catholic Edition. This edition of Sacred Scripture is both accurate and readable. The RSV translation is used in this book.

The Jerusalem Bible. Valuable for its notes and introductions.

The New American Bible. This translation and edition was sponsored by the Bishops' Committee of the Confraternity of Christian Doctrine.

Gospel Parallels: A Synopsis of the First Three Gospels, with alternative readings from the manuscripts and noncanonical parallels (3rd. rev. ed. Camden, 1967).

R.S.V. Interlinear Greek English New Testament, the Nestle Greek text with a literal English translation (3rd. rev. ed., London, 1975).

Horizontal Line Synopsis of the Gospels, RSV text, (Dillsboro, 1975).

Enchiridion Biblicum. Documenta ecclesiastica Sacram Scripturam spectantia auctoritate Pontificiae Commissionis de Re Biblica edita (4th ed. enlarged and revised, Rome, repr. 1965).

The Jerome Biblical Commentary, ed. R. Brown et al (Englewood Cliffs, N.J., 1969).

A New Catholic Commentary of Holy Scriptures, ed. R. Fuller *et al* (London, 1969).

A Catholic Commentary on Holy Scripture, ed. B. Orchard *et al* (London, 1953).

Bauer, J.B., ed., *Sacramentum Verbi* 3 Vols. (New York, 1970).

Daniel-Rops, H., *What is the Bible?* (Vol. 60 of the Twentieth Century Encyclopedia of Catholicism; New York, 1958).

Hartman L., ed., *Encyclopedic Dictionary of the Bible* (New York, 1963).

Leon-Dufour, X., *Dictionary of Biblical Theology* (2nd rev. ed., New York, 1973).

McKenzie, J., *Dictionary of the Bible* (Milwaukee, 1965).

For the Fathers of the Church a manual such as the three-volume work *Patrology* by Johannes Quasten (Westminster, 1960) would be most helpful as it also indicates other works that should be consulted. The Migne collection of the Fathers ought to be in a library to which the student has ready access. This collection contains all the works of the Latin and Greek Fathers in two series. The works were first put together, edited and published by Father Jacques Paul Migne between 1844 and 1866. It remains the standard source book for the Fathers even though individual volumes have been surpassed by later, more critical editions.

The following are standard works with which the scholar should be familiar:

Patrologiae cursus completus, series latina, ed. J.P. Migne, 221 vols. (Paris 1844–1855).

Patrologiae cursus completus, series graeca, ed. J.P. Migne, 161 vols. (Paris 1857–1866).

Sources chretiennes (Paris, 1941–   ).

Corpus Christianorum, series latina (Turnhout-Paris, 1953–   ).

Corpus Christianorum, series graeca (Turnhout-Paris, 1974–   ).

Library of the Fathers, 45 vols. (Oxford, 1838–1888).

The Ante-Nicene Christian Library, 24 vols. (Edinburgh, 1866–1872), with a supplementary vol. (Edinburgh, 1897).

The Ante-Nicene Fathers, 8 vols. (Buffalo, 1884–1886). American rev. reprint of the Edinburgh edition, with two supplementary volumes (9 and 10). Repr. Grand Rapids, 1955ff.

A Select Library of Nicene and Post-Nicene Fathers of the Christian Church, 28 vols. (Buffalo and New York, 1886–1900). Repr. Grand Rapids, 1951ff.

Ancient Christian Writers, ed. J. Quasten *et al.* (New York-Washington, D.C., 1947–).

Library of Christian Classics, ed. J. Baillie *et al.* (London and Philadephia, 1953–   ).

Ancient Christian Writers, ed. J. Quasten *et al.* (Westminster, Md., — London — New York — Paramus, N.J., 1946–   ).

The Fathers of the Church, ed. R.J. Deferrari *et al. 67 vols.* (New York — Washington, D.C., 1947–   ).

The Library of Christian Classics, ed. J. Baille *et al.* (London and Philadelphia, 1953–   ).

Oxford Early Christian Texts (New York, 1971–   ). Rouet de Journel, M.J., *Enchiridion Patristicum* (24th ed., Barcinon — Freiburg — Rome — New York, Herder, 1969).

Wuerl, D., *Fathers of the Church* (Boston, 1982). A short, popular introduction to the Fathers.

For the study of theology, another basic source is the Magisterium. The student should seek out these texts in their original form and not in an edited or abridged translation. The basic source book for magisterial texts is the so-called Denzinger. The most recent edition of this is: H. Denzinger, A. Schönmetzer, *Enchiridion Symbolorum Definitionum et Declarationum de Rebus Fidei et Morum* (36th ed. emended, Freiburg, 1976). To this should be added the documents of Vatican Council II and subsequent documents of the

Holy See. The *Enchiridion Vaticanum* in 6 volumes (Bologna, 1966–) provides the original text not only of the Council documents but also all other official documents of the Holy See from 1963 up to and including those issued in 1979.

The following works provide access to the magisteral texts:

Official texts of documents issued by the Holy Father and the Sacred Congregations of the Holy See are published in *Acta Apostolicae Sedis* (Rome, 1909–), the predecessor of which was the *Acta Sanctae Sedis* (Rome, 1865–1908).

The Documents of Vatican II, ed. M. W. Abbott (New York, 1966). and *Vatican Council II: The Conciliar and Post-Conciliar Documents* ed. A. Flannery (Northport, N.Y., 1975).

The Teachings of the Second Vatican Council: Complete Texts of the Constitutions, Decrees and Declarations (Westminster, Md., 1966).

Vatican II Documents (Glenrock, N.J., 1965).

Conciliorum Oecumenicorum Decreta, ed. Centro di Documentazione, Istituto per le Scienze Religiose, Bologna (Barcelona — Freiburg — Rome, 1962).

The Church Teaches, Documents of the Church in English Translation (St. Louis, Mo., 1955).

The Teaching of the Catholic Church, originally prepared by J. Neuner and H. Roos, ed. by K. Rahner trans. by G. Steven from the original German (Staten Island, N.Y., 1967).

The Christian Faith in the Doctrinal Documents of the Catholic Church, ed. J. Neune and J. Dupuis (rev. ed. Westminster, Md., 1975).

The best work on the Synod of Bishops' meetings is not available in English. *Il Sinodo dei Vescovi,* G. Caprile, S. J. (Rome, 1967–78, 6 vols.).

To this list of specialized reference works we add the following general reference material and conclude with a few titles of popularized works that can well serve as an introduction to the Fathers, Theology, or Church History for one just beginning to approach the world of theological thought and development:

Eusebius, *History of the Church* (Baltimore; Penguin Books, 1965). This version is an inexpensive and available text of Eusebius.

Enchiridion Fontium Historiae Ecclesiasticae Antiquae, quod collegit C. Kirch (8th ed., Barcinone, 1960).

Daniel-Rops, H., *History of the Church of Christ,* 10 vols. (New York, 1957–1967). Vol. 1: *The Church of the Apostles and Martyrs* (1960); vol. 2: *The Church in the Dark Ages* (1959); vol. 3: *Cathedral and Crusade: Studies of the Medieval Church* (1957); vol. 4: *The Protestant Reformation* (1961); vol. 5: *The Catholic Reformation* (1962); vol. 6: *The Church in the Seventeenth Century* (1963); vol. 7: *The Church in the Eighteenth Century* (1964); vol. 8: *The Church in an Age of Revolution, 1789–1870* (1965); vol. 9: *A Fight for God* (1966); vol. 10: *Our Brothers in Christ* (1967).

Harney M. P., *The Catholic Church through the Ages* (Boston, 1974).

Hughes, P., *A History of the Church,* 3 vols. (London, 1934–47).

Hughes, P., *A Popular History of the Catholic Church* (New York, 1947, 1954).

Hughes, P., *The Church in Crisis: A History of the General Councils, 325–1870* (New York, 1961).

Mourrett, F., *History of the Catholic Church,* 8 vols. (trans. by N. Thompson; St. Louis, 1931, 1957).

The following are general reference materials:

Bouyer, L., *Dictionary of Theology* (trans. by C. Quinn; New York, 1966).

Cross, F. L., and Livingstone, E. A., eds., *The Oxford Dictionary of the Christian Church* (2nd ed., New York, 1974).

Lawler, R., Wuerl, D., Lawler, T., *The Teaching of Christ* (Huntington, 1976).

New Catholic Encyclopedia, 15 vols. (New York, 1967). Vol. 16, Supplement 1967–74 (1974); Vol. 17 Supplement 1975–78 (1979).

Rahner, K., ed. *Sacramentum Mundi,* 6 vols. (New York, 1968–70).

Rahner, K., ed. *Encyclopedia of Theology, the Concise Sacramentum Mundi* (New York, 1975).

Rahner, K., and Vorgrimler, H., *Theological Dictionary* (New York, 1965).

St. Thomas Aquinas, *Summa Theologica,* 3 vols. (New York, 1947–48). English Translation of the *Summa Theologica.*

St. Thomas Aquinas, *Summa Theologica,* ed. T. Gilby and T. C. O'Brien, New York, 1964). This series includes original text, translation and extensive notes To be completed in sixty volumes.

St. Thomas Aquinas, *On the Truth of the Catholic Faith,* 5 vols.

(trans. by A. C. Pegis *et al;* New York, 1955–1957. A translation of St. Thomas' *Summa contra Gentiles.*

Basic Writings of Saint Thomas Aquinas, ed. and annot. A. C. Pegis, 2 vols. (New York, 1945): includes transations of the *Summa Theologica* I, 1–119, I–II, 6–114; II–II, 1–7; and of the *Summa contra Gentiles* III, 1–113.

Vorgrimler, H., ed., *Commentry on the Documents of Vatican II,* 5 vols. (New York, 1967).

Study Program

For the first years of theological study, we recommend a rotation in the subjects chosen for deeper study, so that the student may have the opportunity to verify every semester his own method regarding use of the individual sources in theology. Toward the end of his studies, and above all after having completed them, it is very useful to *specialize in some aspect* of theological work. The specialization can be carried out following two main lines. The first is the choice of a branch of the theological sources: e.g., the student can choose as the favorite subject of his studies some book of Sacred Scripture (Psalms, Gospels, St. Paul, St John), some Church Father (Augustine, Ambrose), or some ancient or modern theologican (St. Thomas, St. Bonaventure, Congar, Rahner), trying to understand better and better the view of the Christian message obtained from a careful study of these works, and rethinking the various questions that he comes across by putting them in the synthesis of these authors.

The second main line for specialization is to choose rather a central theological subject (the figure of Jesus, the Cross, the Resurrection, the Holy Spirit, the Church), trying to determine the development of this subject in the various theological sources, and considering the various events of Christian life in the light of the central mystery chosen.

Both these specializations become harmful when exclusive, so that the student rejects all thought alien to the perspective of the author he has studied, or takes no interest in any question in which he does not see a connection with the mystery chosen. If, on the contrary the specialization becomes a center of crystallization for a synthesis open to the whole field of theological thought, it will be an extraordinary effective means to reach maturity of thought, and will reveal ever new depths also for the ministry of the world. The more one knows the mind of a great theologian, or the riches hidden in some central mystery, the easier it will be to say deep, true, living, and new things, in the many circumstances of pastoral life. Among our former pupils groups of priests have been formed who, living together and exercising the parish ministry together, have chosen different specializations and taken a university degree in them, just to be able to attain a more structured spiritual, cultural, and operational unity.

Reading

The reading of theological publications has always been of prime importance in the study of theology, but the development of the publishing industry today has deeply changed the function of reading in these studies as a whole.

Even several centuries after the invention of printing, a cultivated person could be content with a few dozen books, and a university was proud to possess some thousands. It was only in the nineteenth century that things changed. However, although reading became an important part of life (personal, family, and national) in the lay world, from the second half of the last century, in the ecclesiastical world, especially in Latin countries, interest in reading new books was not felt from some time. This depended on different causes, some material (the secularization of ecclesiastic property), some cultural (hostility toward the new), some religious (mistrust regarding the value of religious studies, caused by the reaction against modernisn). Visiting the libraries of seminaries, one sees that they stopped buying new books at the end of the nineteenth century. The archaic equipment of the libraries also shows that they constituted a territory extraneous to everyday life. Rarely was a sum assigned annually in the budget of seminaries to be spent on new books, and the office of libraries was one of the many tasks of some elderly, cultivated ecclesiastic. The consequences of this mentality was that the average ecclesiastic was content with a library reduced to the minimum, in which dogmatic theology was represented at most by manuals kept from his seminary days.

In the cultural climate of that time, the didactic and methodological concern of those who wishes to raise the level of studies was to arouse curiosity, make people appreciate books, and bring new books and reviews into the cultural horizon of the clergy, in brief, to increase the *quantity* of reading.

Today that situation has changed. The publishing world has turned its attention to theology, religion, and ethics. The quantity of such works and their availability have risen strongly in the years following the Council. These books are mainly interested in Christian action in the world. Their doctrinal value varies a great deal. In this new situation there is a danger that the theologian may indeed read a great deal, but badly, that is, without choosing, in an unmethodical, superficial, and hurried way.

One reads *without choosing* when one picks up a book without considering its inner value and its function for one's intellectual development. One reads in an *unmethodical* way when one takes no interest in the cultural environment from which the author comes and therefore does not exactly understand his language. One reads in a *superficial* way when one does not take the trouble to decipher objectively the author's message, but appreciates the reading only because of its stimulating value for one's own subjective thought. One reads in a *hurried* way when one does not record the contribution of the book, so that as soon as one has finished reading, its contents vanishes from one's mind.

These dangers are real and serious ones. Therefore, though we do not want to repeat the paradoxical advice to read little in order to read well, we think that in the flood of mediocre publications, the theologian must organize his reading in order to improve its *quality*.

In the first place it is necessary to choose well what one reads, planning it in such a way that no semester will pass without the student reading some fundamental work, referring to the subject he is studying, according to the plan of studies of his seminary or faculty. These books may not be easy or inviting, but some sector of theological literature refers to them continually, as the classic foundation of present-day research. It is not a good thing, for example, to complete one's theological studies without having read anything of authors such as von Balthasar, Congar, de Lubac, Rahner, Schillebeeckx, and Tillich. After completing his studies, the theologian must be urged in the first place to follow with equal perseverance some review that will keep him up to date in the world of studies. At present, the "Nouvelle Revue Theologique" is to be recommended particularly; in its articles and reviews it gives ample and deep information without going into subtleties that interest only a very few technicians.

In English the international reviews available include *Angelicum*, *Communio*, *Concilium*, *Gregorianum*, *Theological Digest*, and *Theological Studies*, as well as more specialized periodicals as *Spiritual Life* and *The Way*.

Priestly collaboration can considerably facilitate access to reviews and periodicals. For example, if the members of a group of five priests each take out a subscription for a review (of spirituality, apostolate, ethics, exegetics, and dogmatics) and circulate the reviews among themselves every week, each of them will find himself in contact with the world of studies without excessive sacrifices. Following the back reviews published in serious periodicals, the theologian will find some new publications corresponding to his specialization every year.

One can avoid being unmethodical in one's reading if one takes care of find out to what cultural context the author belongs. When it is a question of writers who are sufficiently well known, the usual works of introduction to theology today offer the necessary information. With regard to other authors who are not so well known, it will be useful to inform oneself on their intellectual background by means of the prefaces (in which the author himself generally gives useful indications), book reviews, etc. It is impossible to understand an author completely until one knows what is the intellectual environment to which he belongs, what are his doctrinal concerns, and what is the starting point he aims at going beyond with his researches. When it is a question of non-Catholic authors, it is particularly important to take into account that certain opinions, which they tacitly presuppose in the course of their studies, are to be explained by the fact that they live in the doctrinal synthesis of another ecclesial community.

Hasty superficiality in reading is a defect difficult to get rid of in our times. To correct it, we must acquire the habit of asking outselves the questions, what exactly is the problem that the author wishes to solve, along what way and on the basis of what certainties does he proceed toward the solution, what are his conclusions, in what way does his position differ from that of other theologians we already know, what is the value of these conclusions, and how may they possibly be applied to solve other problems that interest us, but which the author has not raised. The habit of taking notes and of making extracts is an effective means not only in order not to forget the fruits of one's reading, but also to read well. An ancient axiom affirmed, "Lectionem sine calamo, temporis perditionem puta." If that is exaggerated, it remains true, however, that one reads in a more mature way when one reads with one's pen in one's hand. It is clear that it is not a question just of copying sentences of the author that strike us particularly; it is more useful, in fact, to try to express that author's thought in our owns words, because that obliges us to assimilate the contents of the book better.

Notes and extracts will be particularly useful when a group of friends forms the habit of meeting every month and each one informs the others about a book he has read, discussing with the others the judgment to be passed on it or the use that can be made of it. It is a good idea, too, to accustom oneself to writing reviews for a magazine. These reviews should not be just an act of courtesy, an advertisement, or a mere summary of the content of the book, but should express also a thought of one's own, in connection with the question dealt with. For many people, the habit of writing such reviews on books recently published on their specialization, has been the beginning of scientific publications that reach wider circles.

Updating

The necessity of periodical updating, in order to be able to exercise any profession well, has always been felt, but today it has become more impelling, owning to the "acceleration of history," that is, the extremely rapid and deep changes that society is undergoing in all areas. It is clear, for example, that a doctor, to be always equal to his task, will have to keep himself constantly informed about the progress of medicine as well an engineer and a teacher. Those activities, moreover, which aim not only at communicating knowledge but also at forming the personality, must not only follow the progress of science, in a given field, but also make me aware of the changes in psychology, tastes, vital requirements, and the environments in which they have to work. Teachers at all levels find themselves in this situation.

The theologian exercises an eminently formative activity. He must contribute to the construction of that building of living stones, which is the Church, not only by making Christ's message known, but also by helping the faithful to live as real disciples of Christ, in the concrete situations of the world of today, so different from those of the world of yesterday.

Hence the necessity of continual updating at a threefold level: (a) to know the progress made in the interpretation of the documents through which Christ's message reaches us (biblical exegesis, history of dogmas, and Christian thought); (b) to know the new problems that concern the faithful and people in general today, since they can be solved in the light of revelation; (c) to know the cultural world of today, its way of thinking and speaking, in order to be able to express oneself and act in such a way as to be understood and to attract listeners effectively to knowledge, love, and service of Christ.

The Council asks repeatedly for continual updating in these three dimensions, both for the laity who are to exercise the apostolate,[17] and for members of the Secular Institutes,[18] and particularly for the clergy.[19]

In the course of this chapter, we indicated various factors of ongoing formation for the theologian. Such are specialization in a source or in a mystery (without which one easily loses taste for continuing studies); extensive updating (following some theological reviews regularly); intensive updating (the analytical reading of recent important works, concerning one's own specialization); the community orientation of studies (the regular meeting of a group, which collaborates also intellectually and discusses conclusions); pastoral orientation (which calls for deeper studies in relation to some more exacting ministries, without which it is easy to lose oneself in the vague and the indefinite).

The Council notes how important it is that updating in theological studies should be intelligently guided by specialists;[20] therefore, precisely in the context of priestly "aggiornamento," it proposes that "some priests devote themselves to deeper study of the sacred sciences" and, as the purpose of this particular specialization indicates, not only teach in seminaries and faculties, but also "ensure that the rest of the priests and the faithful will be helped to acquire the knowledge of religion necessary for them."[21]

An important ministry, which professional theologians must exercise, consists, in fact, in the help given to their confreres who, more involved in direct pastoral care, have less time to dedicate to study.

Experience has taught us that it is opportune to organize organic courses, with well-chosen teachers, who are really anxious to help their confreres to find their way in the present crisis. The teachers, therefore, must not aim at causing a stir, presenting themselves as those who come at last to proclaim the new word, with regard to which everything that has been taught previously must be rejected. On the contrary they must be concerned to show how the present developments in the various areas of the sacred sciences are in continuity with the teaching of the Church, although they lead to considering new problems or new aspects of old problems that call for new solutions today, solutions that, perhaps, have not yet been found.

It is also important that teachers, despite the inevitable pluralism, should not differ on fundamentals (so that, for example, one considers the positions of the other as a danger for faith, either in the progressive direction or in the conservative one); otherwise the course, instead of guiding, would bring greater confusion.

A renewal course must not, of course, be reduced to a series of lectures listened to more or less patiently. Continual dialogue between teachers and participants is necessary. In this dialogue the theoretical specialist can be greatly helped to understand better that doctrine in which he is competent, when he is put in contact with practical aspects, which priests engaged directly in pastoral care know better than he does. In order that the mutual collaboration between teachers and participants should obtain its whole effect, it will be useful for the participants to form working groups. These groups will not aim in the first place at going more deeply into the doctrine set forth, from the speculative point of view, but rather at examining how it can be presented to the faithful in catechesis, and what impact it has on the Christian life of everyone.

Without denying the importance of courses organized to last for a certain number of years, it is very useful, during the summer, to organize intensive courses lasting for a week on a given subject. We have often taken part in courses of this type, with very good results, not only from the intellectual point of view, but also because of the mutual encouragement we give one another, living together for some days for the purpose of becoming better instruments to make Christ known and loved. It seems opportune to organize courses in such a way that they are addressed mainly (not exclusively) either to the older clergy (who completed their theological studies before the Council) or to the younger clergy (post conciliar). In fact, the problems of the two generations are different. In neither case is it sufficient to set forth the results of theological studies; it is necessary to help them to engage in theological work, with continual critical updating of what they learned in the course of their studies. It must be driven home to the older ones that faithfulness to the "deposit" does not exclude but on the contrary demands the continual search for new formulas, which do not contradict but complete the partial truth of ancient formulas, expressing better the meaning of the identical message.

The problems of the younger ones, on the other hand, are closer to those of fundamental theology. They must be helped to understand how the central data of faith correspond to the requirements deeply felt by the environment, so much so that precisely the serious desire for human advancement postulates adherence to the mystery of

Christ, acceptance of the Church, and continuity with that historical movement that spread from Christ through the Apostles and the Church Fathers, creating Christianity, such as we know it. This is done in both cases by highlighting the central mysteries of faith, and the connection that the various truths have with Christ, the foundation and center of faith,[22] which is not a reduction, but a concentration of it and a structuring of the message. Therefore the result of these renewal courses will not be so much to prove or clarify particular assertions, but to strengthen intelligent and critical adherence to the ecclesial message, understood as a historical fact, that is, at once permanent and changeable.

In the six-day courses, the following program gave good results: three hours of work morning and afternoon, consisting of one hour's lecture, one hour's group work, and one hour's discussion of the results in common. The group work is more fruitful if "professional" theologians are present as animators in each group. They can solve any misunderstandings that arise without bringing them to the general assembly, suggest documentation for the discussions, and formulate the questions of the group precisely and concisely.

To give participants a complete stenciled text of the lectures calls for too much work and considerable expense, outweighing the usefulness. It is necessary, on the other hand, to give schemata, which give help in following the lectures, and guide the group work, and bibliographical and methodological indications, for private study to be continued later. This study will be the most important result of the course, and the real architect of continual "aggiornamento."

Research

We conclude this chapter with a glance at the highest level of theological study, that is, research properly speaking, in which it is a question not just of acquiring or spreading a doctrine already found and proved by others, but of bringing about the progress of theological science by discovering new aspects of the message of salvation.

It would be a mistake to think that scientific investigation is an activity reserved for exceptional people. The excessively long duration of theological studies (it takes at least eight years to obtain a degree in theology, while only four are necessary in arts), easily gives rise to this misunderstanding, since it reduces the scholar to a perpetual student, who never dares to propose an opinion under his own responsibility, but confines himself to repeating lectures in which a doctrine is sustained or contested. It is therefore necessary to stress that a well-directed "seminar," a "deeper study," which is the fruit of the. latter, and especially the teaching, normally lead the scholar to some personal discovery, and there is no reason why he should not communicate his discoveries also to others, not only by talking, preaching, and teaching, but also by writing, if not at once a book, at least an article in a specialized review. The more frequent publication of degree theses, and even more of studies made after obtaining the doctorate, would produce an open and stimulating cultural atmosphere, advantageous for theological life in the widest sense.

The studies, the results of which are communicated and verified in publications, are often and opportunely concerned with problems really raised in the local Church. Even scholars of high repute use such opportunities for their publications: for researchers not yet accustomed to active and fully responsible theological study, that is even more advisable because it avoids approaching the theological study on a plane of abstraction, unrelated to the life of the community.

In the second place, the literary genre known as the "contribution" is to be recommended. It is a mistake to think that only the complete solution of a whole set of problems is worth publishing. This solution is normally the fruit of various partial contributions. The contribution may assume various forms. To mention some examples that are more easily accessible, it may aim at the interpretation of a source (a biblical theme, the work of a Father of the Church, of a council, etc.), adding to the image so far elaborated an observation made from a new point of view.

It may seek to illuminate some aspect of the revealed mystery (the Trinity, the Church, salvation) by drawing upon some theological source that has not been sufficiently considered so far; it may pursue a further understanding of faith, based on the doctrinal proposals of a scholar, of which it gives an ample review, examining their validity and developing further virtualities. Finally it is also very useful to publish a bibliographical report on a particular branch of theological studies, particularly if it is not only complete in the enumeration of the various publications, but also accompanied by explanatory and critical observations that transform the mere material documentation into a personal view of an aspect of the theological movement.

The critical nature of the study, that is, concern to verify every assertion and every step of the reasoning, is essential in scientific research. This means that the author puts at the reader's disposal the means to check the accuracy of every affirmation that is not already accepted in the cultural environment of the publication.

The critical method in theology moves in the first place on the philological plane, since it refers to the historiologically correct use of documents emerging from the past (Bible, writings of the Church Fathers, documents of the Magisterium). The philologico-historical verification has three main forms. The author explains how his affirmation follows from truths already admitted by the readers, or from affirmations that have already been verified; he indicates the sources on which the affirmation is based; he cites the works that contain the scientific verification of the respective affirmations on the basis of the sources.

In theology, and particularly in dogmatic theology, however, in addition to philologico-historical criticism, another criticism, the hermeneutical one, is also necessary. The latter neutralizes (mostly with the procedures of linguistic analysis) the image of the world (understood as a complete view of the universe) in which the message of the sources is delivered, to the extent that it is not postulated by that message, and it expresses the message of the sources, in the present-day view of the world, to the extent to which this view is compatible with the message.

To effect the criticism not only with regard to the accuracy of facts but also with regard to the choice of premises, the validity of explanations and in noetic procedures, scientific thought needs a philosophy, not so much in the sense of a metaphysic, as rather in that of an instrument of thought. The delicate point of theological research today lies here. The conviction still existed in the first half of the century that theological reflection has its foundations in metaphysics and in scholastic epistemology. At present, after the failure of the neo-Thomist restoration, theological reflection finds itself in a void, which is sometimes accepted with agnostic references, sometimes apparently filled with the utilization of philosophical trends that have not been proved compatible with the Christian message (e.g., neopositivism, Marxism, existentialism).[23]

Hermeneutical criticism postulates, therefore, a new gnosiological vehicle, which will replace the scholastic system, and in which the acculturation of the message of the sources can take place. Therefore the most active and interesting (and also most difficult) branch of theological research will be the working out of a philosophy that, probably, will no longer be considered a system of truths, established independently of faith, which serves as a propaedeutic for the science of faith, but rather as a set of assertions postulated by faith and thought with the gnosiological means used in the present cultural environment, which will permit a dialogue of faith with the philosophies and ideologies of the environment.

The elaboration of assertions postulated by the sources but expressed in the language of the cultural environment, carried out with the procedures of a critical hermeneutics, is the only means to avoid interpretations lacking critically established criteria, which transform theology into ideology. We mean here by "ideology" a system of thought in which the criterion of assent depends on what is asserted with regard to a "cause" (e.g., the consolidation of the contestation of an institution), so that the gnosiological value of the premises, the confrontation with empirical experience, the recourse to the sources, lose importance or are manipulated. This happens when one documents a series of facts philologically and historically, but passes over in silence the reason why those data and not others are put forward, when certain aspects of the data are considered instead of others, when data are connected and explained by means of an explicative principle not proved nor even stated.

The ideologization of theology tends above all to polarize studies in two dynamic the diametrically opposed systems, according to the tacitly admitted interpretative principle that theological truth is the one that strengthens, or else destroys, a sociological institution (of the state, the Church, etc.). Thus theology becomes "political," not only in the acceptable sense of taking into account the political implications of faith, but also in the unacceptable sense of interpreting faith in virtue of political options.

Let us admit, if you like, that any cultural content, and therefore also any theological discourse, has inevitably a political charge, since in actual fact it is useful or harmful with regard to a given way of constructing community life. In this sense it is perhaps true that no human attitude, and so not even theological research, can in actual fact be politically neutral. But neutrality in actual fact is one thing, and neutrality of intention is another. The latter consists in the methodical policy of choosing the doctrinal positions that seem postulated by the sources and therefore true, regardless of the possibility that these positions may possibly be exploited by some political force.

Of course, the method of "neutrality of intention," which contradicts any tendency insofar as it is opposed to the word of God and accepts any tendency insofar as it is in conformity with this word, is in permanent conflict with all ideology that, absolutizing itself, demands an acritical and total adherence.

Therefore scientifically critical theological research implies an existential attitude which is prompted by living faith.

With this final observation, there reappears the conception of the theological method that has permeated our whole essay right from the beginning. One engages in theology, insofar as one lives a truly Christian existence also on the intellectual side, interpreting critically the ecclesial reality, according to the requirements of the word of God, in the epistemological context of one's own cultural environment.

CHAPTER NOTES

1. Cf. *Apostolicam actuositatem*, n. 3; Vatican Council II, *Decree on the Apostolate of the Laity*, (November 18, 1965).

2. *Der Spiegel*, December 24, 1973, p. 40.

3. Cf. *S. Th.*, Prologus; Bonaventura, *Breviloquim*, Prologus 6 (Op. 5,208).

4. We made such a comparison in the monograph *Nova creatura* (Rome, 1957), which gathers the doctrine on grace from the medieval commentaries on St. Paul.

5. On the level of practical application, it is instructive to consult *The Report of the Biships' Ad Hoc Committee for Priestly Life and Ministry*, United States Catholic Conference, (Washington 1974); *The Theological Formation of Future Priests*, Sacred Congregation for Catholic Education (Rome, 1976); *Philosophy in Priestly Formation* ed. Ronald Lawler, Catholic University of America (Washington, 1978).

6. For the structure of medieval universities, cf. H. Rashdall, F. M. Powiche, A. B. Emden, *The Universities of Europe in the Middle Ages* (ed. 2, Oxford, 1936); L. Thorndike, *University Records and Life in the Middle Ages* (New York, 1944); D. Knowles, *The Evolution of Medieval Thought* (London, 1962); R. R. Bolgar, *The Classical Heritage* (New York, 1954).

7. From the immense literature that exists on this subject, we mention for general information A. P. Hare, *Handbook of Small Group Research* (ed. 6, New York, 1967); W. M. Lifton, *Working with Groups* (ed. 2, New York, London, Sidney, 1966); H. A. Thelen, *Dynamics of Groups at Work* (ed. 8, Chicago, London, 1967); M. Sader, B. Clemens-Lodge, H. Keil-Specht, A. Weingarten, *Klein Fibel zum Hochschulunterricht* (München, 1970); F. Kaspar, *Gruppenpädagogische Unterrichtsverfahren für den Religionsunterricht* (Stuttgart, München, 1971).

8. Mansi 49, pp. 653–55; 731; 739–42.

9. Mansi 50, pp. 59–60; 68; 76; 102–103; 122–25; 138–147; Mansi 53, 159–161.

10. Mansi 51, pp. 33; 37; 45–46; 101–102; 107–112.

11. For the terminology *otium, quies, vigiliae, meditatio, lectio, intellectus, quaestio,* etc., cf. J. Leclercq, *Etudes sur le vocabulaire monastique du moyen age* (Rome,

1961); *Otia monastica* (Rome, 1963); *Amour des lettres et le desir de Dieu* (Paris, 1957); M. Chenu, *Nature, Man, and Society in the 12th Century* (Chicago, 1968).

12. A.D. Sertillanges, *The Intellectual Life: Its Spirit and Conditions* (Westminster, Md., 1948).

13. A useful and up-to-date series of theological manuals is the six-volume *Dogma* set by Michael Schmaus: *Dogma 1, God in Revelation* (Kansas City, 1968); *Dogma 2, God and Creation* (1969); *Dogma 3, God and His Christ* (1971); *Dogma 4, The Church* (1972); *Dogma 5, The Church as Sacrament* (1975); and *Dogma 6, Justification and the Last Things* (1977).

14. Document of the International Theological Commission on *Unity of Faith and Theological Pluralism* in *La Civiltà Cattolica* 124 (1973/II); for the explanation of this statement cf. M. Flick, "Chiesa permissiva o Chiesa repressiva?" in *ibid.* (1973/II, pp. 457–58).

15. *Optatam totius,* n. 16.

16. Matt. 22:31–32; Mark 12:26–27; Luke 20:37–38; cf. F. Dreyfus, "L'arqument scripturaire de Jésus en faveur de la résurrection des morts" in: *Revue Biblique* 66 (1959) pp. 213–24.

17. Cf. the necessity of "formatio semper perficienda" (a steadily perfected formation), in *Apostolicam actuositam,* n. 29.

18. Cf. the postulate of "ulterior formatio promovenda" (a more advanced formation), in *Perfectae caritatis,* n. 11; Vatican Council II, *Decree on the Renewal of Religious Life,* (October 28, 1965).

19. *Presbyterorum ordinis,* n. 19; Vatican Council II, *Decree on the Life and Ministry of Priests* (December 7, 1965), not only reminds bishops that "incitantur Presbyteri ut scientiam suam de divinis et humanis apte et sine intermissione perficiant" (Priests are urged to adequate and continuous perfection of their knowledge of things divine and human) but also sketches a program of this ongoing formation of the clergy, and recommends that the institutional conditions should be realized, such as courses and congresses, study centers, libraries, personnel in charge of specialized studies, etc. Cf. also the *Letter of the Congregation for the Clergy to the Presidents of the Episcopal Conferences, on ongoing formation of the clergy in the world today,* in *AAS* 62 (1970) pp. 123–34.

20. *Presbyterorum ordinis,* n, 19, "apta per personas idoneas studiorum moderatio" (the proper direction of studies by suitable persons).

21. *Ibid.*

22. *Unitatis redintegratio,* n. 11.

23. The phenomenon can already be observed in the vagueness with which Vatican II speaks of the function of philosophy in priestly formation (*Optatam totius,* n. 15), and it is examined in the *Circular of the Congregation for Catholic education* on January 20, 1972; also cf: *Philosophy in Priestly Formation,* ed. Ronald Lawler (Washington, 1978).